Success In Many Shades

Other books edited by Teresa Allissa Citro

Parenting the Child with Learning Disabilities: The Experts Speak

Successful Lifetime Management:Adults with Learning Disabilities

*Transition Skills for Post-Secondary Success:
Reflections for High School Students with Learning Disabilities*

Success In Many Shades:

A Spectrum of Post-Secondary Options

Edited by

Teresa Allissa Citro
Executive Director
Learning Disabilities Worldwide

Learning Disabilities
Worldwide

This book is dedicated to Kim Button, Rob Crosby and Tony Cunis. You are exceptional! I can't wait to see all your dreams come true. You are heroes!

—Teresa A. Citro—

Contents

FOREWORD

Transitions . . . decisions . . . transition . . . decisions . . .
transition...decisions . . . transition . . .

For parents, advocates and professionals who work with people with learning disabilities, it often seems that the transition/decision/transition cycle is a perpetual lifestyle. As the person with LD grows and matures, he goes through an ongoing series of transitions (preschool-to-kindergarten, kindergarten to grade school, grade school to middle school, etc.) and each of these transitions requires that decisions be made. The larger the transition, the more critical the decision.

However, there is no transition that is greater or more significant than the transition from high school to post secondary programs or the work force. The adolescent has struggled diligently—along with his support system of parents and professionals—to receive his high school diploma. Now, placement decisions must be made that will enable the graduate to utilize his hard earned skills. A placement error at this critical juncture can be devastating and can have a long-term impact upon the person's self-esteem, motivation and quality of life.

Post secondary placements should present the student with a challenging workload and curriculum . . . but, should also offer and provide the support and structure that is fundamental to success.

It is quite ironic that, in a true sense, the *real world* is kinder to the Learning Disabled person than is the world of *school*. The experience of many practitioners in our field has shown that the workplace is far more accommodating than is the classroom for the person with special needs. In many cases, post-secondary education truly offers the young adult with a learning disability a "second chance".

There are many reasons why this is true. Primary among them is the structure of Secondary Schools within the United States today. Most high schools celebrate the *generalist*. The student who receives "all A's" is the student who becomes Valedictorian. High schools celebrate the student who is equally good in Science, Mathematics, Foreign Languages and Social Sciences. This is a student whom we all assume will succeed and will have a bright and promising future. However, we then send students out into the real world where it is the *specialist,* not the generalist, who most often succeeds.

Society's need for specialists provides a second chance for the learning disabled young adult to become a useful part of the adult community. The real world demands that you be talented at *something,* not at *everything.* Once a young adult has found a vocation that matches skills and interest, he is able to enjoy the success that has often eluded him during his high school years.

Dr. Samuel Kirk coined the term Learning Disability in 1962. It is often referred to as the "hidden handicap" because there is generally no outward appearance of the disability. Young adults with learning disabilities generally appear to be no different than their non-disabled peers.

It is estimated that 6 to 10 percent of the population of the United States is learning disabled. Nearly 40 percent of the children enrolled in the nation's Special Education classes suffer from learning disabilities. The National Center for Learning Disabilities estimates that there are six million adults with disabilities including a significant portion of the workforce.

Many students with learning disabilities have superior intellect. These students are able to devise ingenious compensatory strategies to bypass their learning difficulties. The students for whom this book is written are generally unable to do this. They must confront their problems directly, and their academic careers present them with many obstacles and struggles. They have often experienced years of failure, misdiagnosis and battered self-esteem. Parents and professionals dealing with this these students must be aware of the challenges they face and must be prepared to provide these young people with a balance of support and challenge. To provide this assistance, it is critically important that we fully understand the nature and the needs of the person with a severe learning disorder.

It is crucial that we begin by presenting a workable definition of this disorder. At the present time, there is great controversy around this issue. Because LD is such a multi-disciplinary field, it is difficult to find a definition that meets the needs and biases of all practitioners and educators. There are nearly 35 accepted definitions of LD and it is highly unlikely that the field will ever arrive at a single definition that will satisfy all those involved in the field.

However, the disparate definitions that exist today have some common factors. Among them are these following:

- There must be a discrepancy between a person's potential for learning and that which the person actually learns.
- There must exist an uneven pattern of development wherein there are significant discrepancies between the person's skills from one area to another.
- The learning problems must not be due primarily to environmental disadvantages, mental retardation or emotional disturbance.

It is wise to utilize a "definition of exclusion when defining a learning disabled population. We should think of the learning disabled young adult as one who is not functioning in school despite the fact that he/she a) is not mentally impaired b) is not emotionally disturbed, c) is not impaired in his modalities, (i.e., blind, deaf) and d) has had an opportunity to learn (i.e., not hindered by excessive school absences, poor teaching, frequent family moves, etc.).

The causes of learning disabilities are also a point of contention in the field. There appears to be no discernable primary cause for the existence of learning disabilities. However, some general observations can be made. For instance, many students' learning disabilities are caused by a "maturational lag" wherein they develop at a slower rate than do their peers. This, of course, creates great difficulty for the student in school. There are many practitioners in the field who feels that this "lag" is not the *cause* of the learning disability, but rather is the *effect*.

Research evidence indicates that some students experience learning disabilities because of injuries before or during the birth process. Inadequate prenatal care has also been cited as a cause and there is an undeniable link between premature births and subsequent learning disabilities. Longitudinal research indicates that learning disabilities tend to run in families and it appears that a genetic link could be a primary cause or factor. This theory is reinforced by the fact that boys tend to comprise the majority of the learning disabled population; however, recent research indicates that the discrepancy between learning disabilities in boys and girls was greatly overstated in the early history of our field.

Although there is great disagreement regarding the definition and the causes of learning disabilities, there is general agreement on the cluster of symptoms that are manifested by people with learning disorders. It is important to note that this symptomology does not disappear in adulthood. The young person whose academic career has been impacted by these behaviors will often continue to manifest them into adulthood. These behaviors create great complications and conflicts for the student in school and these complications often persist into the workplace. Among the most significant symptoms are:

- **Poor performance on group tests.** This is a significant limitation for a young adult attempting to enter the workforce. Many companies and corporations require group tests and post-secondary programs often insist that such exams be taken during the high school years. The student's performance on these tests is often not reflective of his true potential and skills.
- **Difficulty discriminating size, shape and color.** Understandably, this deficiency creates difficulty for the child who is attempting to

learn to read; however, it can persist in adulthood and this makes seemingly mundane vocational tasks quite difficult for the young adult with a learning disability.

- **Difficulty with temporal (time) concepts.** Many children with learning disabilities have difficulty learning how to tell time and also dealing with temporal concepts of time estimation, planning, etc. Again, these difficulties often continue into adulthood and impact upon the person's ability to deal with day-to-day activities.

- **Distorted concept of body image.** There was a time in our field that the LD child was referred to as "the clumsy child". They often experience difficulty in fine motor skills and are unable to integrate the visual and motor skills simultaneously. This disability would cause great difficulty in mastering tasks such as sorting, keyboard usage, etc.

- **Hyperactivity.** One of the most common traits for the person with learning disabilities is the maintenance of appropriate activity for a situation. These people are often described as "restless" and have difficulty sitting still or staying on task.

- **Slowness in completing work.** People with learning disabilities have a difficult time with memory tasks and are often unable to master repetitive tasks that are easily learned by others. For instance, the reader will doubtless find that you can brush your teeth in the dark with little difficulty. Because this act has been ingrained in the neurological system in such a way that it requires little thought to complete. For young adults with learning disabilities, these repetitive tasks are often not integrated into the neurological system and, therefore, each time they attempt the task it seems new and unfamiliar to them.

- **Poor organizational skills.** Because of the lack of integration and processing skills, many learning disabled young adults have a very difficult time ordering themselves and their environment. They appear to be in a state of constant confusion. This creates great stress for the person and has a negative impact on his ability to function in the workplace or social settings.

- **Easily confused by directions or instructions.** Because of the language disorder and the lack of processing skills, it is often difficult for the LD young adult to understand and follow directions.

- **Difficulty with abstract reasoning and/or problem solving.** This is another example of a lack of language skills having a marked impact on the person's ability to function. Many learning disabled young adults have difficulty with abstract or conceptual thinking and therefore are unable to generate diverse solutions to a problem. Because the person has often failed at such tasks, he tends to be reluctant to take the initiative in situations and will often ask for help when it is unnecessary.

- **Perseveration.** This is a neurologically based characteristic wherein the LD young adult will focus on one topic at the exclusion of all others. He is often unaware that he is doing this and is equally unaware that this exclusivity is not socially acceptable.
- **Difficulty with long term or short term memory.** Memory is receiving tremendous attention in the field of learning disabilities today and a lack of skill in this area will impact negatively on a person's ability to function in the workplace. Oftentimes the learning disabled adult will have a memory that is totally unselective. That is, she is never sure of what information is important enough to be processed into long-term memory and which information should be dismissed because it is unimportant or inconsequential. She remembers the "trees" and forgets the "forest".
- **Impulsive behavior.** Some young adults with learning disabilities have little reflective thought prior to action. They will approach a task and attempt to complete it before making the necessary planning.
- **Low tolerance for frustration.** Because of a number of factors common to learning disabled young adults, they often have a low tolerance for frustration, failure and repetitive tasks. In the early years of vocational education it was felt that people with learning problems should be assigned repetitive, mundane tasks to complete. It was felt that their "lack of intelligence" enabled them to be satisfied with such tedious tasks. We now know that the converse is true and these people are not particularly skilled at tasks that are repetitive or mundane.
- **Poor peer relationships.** It is widely accepted that learning disabled people have as much difficulty mastering social skills as they do mastering academic skills. In fact, research indicates that learning disabled adults who are unable to enjoy success in society, generally fail because of lack of social skills, not their lack of academic prowess. Their impulsivity and their language problems make it difficult for them to relate to peers at an appropriate level.
- **Poor adjustment to environmental changes.** The learning disabled adult often finds it difficult to deal with transitions or changes in his environment. Even a minor change in the workplace setting can create great stress and anxiety for this person.

This must be seriously considered when a student is being trained for a specific vocation or occupation.

- **Difficulty with tasks requiring sequencing.** Such tasks are very difficult for many young adults with learning disabilities because they are often unable to discern a sequence and follow it.

It is important to realize that *none* of the above listed symptoms occur in *every* learning disabled adult. Some LD young adults will suffer from a cluster of these symptoms and some will experience only one. There are no symptoms that are common to all learning disabled people–and all of us suffer from some of these symptoms at times. The significant difference is that the learning disabled person suffers from these difficulties in a chronic and uncontrolled manner.

It is equally important to consider that although these problems create great challenges and obstacles for the LD young adult, they do *not* preclude successful involvement in the workplace or post-secondary programs. The key factor is that the student must be guided and assisted to find an occupation that meets both his *skills* and *interests*. When I was in high school, I underwent a mandatory series of vocational tests. The results indicated that I should investigate a career as a telephone lineman. It seems that these test results showed that I had the skills that would be required for such an occupation. However, the battery never considered my *interests.* I happen to be rather sedentary in my lifestyle and do not particularly enjoy being outdoors. I could not imagine spending my life climbing telephone poles, oftentimes in harsh weather. In this particular example, my *skills* were considered, but not my *interests.* I am sure most of us have had similar experiences.

In my career, I have often consulted with Rehabilitation Counselors. These professionals are responsible for conferring with young adults with learning disabilities in an effort to determine their ultimate vocational placements. It is often reported to me that learning disabled young adults have a very unrealistic idea of their vocational potential. For example, a learning disabled young adult may enter a Rehabilitation Office with dreams and hopes of being a surgeon, airline pilot or television news anchor. These goals are unobtainable for that person and it falls to the counselor to guide the client away from these overambitious goals. The fact that the learning disabled young adult may hold these unrealistic vocational goals is rooted in two factors; a) the person may be unaware of the complexity and the demands of the profession that he is considering and b) the person's parents may have allowed him to live with these unrealistic goals in a well-intentioned attempt to allow the student "his dreams".

We often find that, in such cases, we must gently "burst the bubble". This is a painful and difficult process for all involved, but it is a necessary one. One of the primary tenets of counseling holds that, "Whenever you take something away from a client, you must give something back." For example, if you decide to teach your young daughter about child molestation, you must realize that you are taking away some of her innocence and peace-of-mind. Therefore, you must be equipped to "give her something back" by providing her with information and guidance as to how she can prevent herself from being molested and, further, what steps to take in the event that such an incident occurred. This is a technique that we must learn to use with learning disabled young adults if we are to counsel them in an effective manner.

Once, while speaking in the Syracuse area, I was approached by a middle-aged couple who told me about their son, Scott. He suffered from a severe learning disability that limited his reading, writing and mathematics skills to elementary school level. He was also exceedingly disorganized and clumsy and had difficulty performing even mundane, integrative tasks. Scott was now 21 years old and wished to become an airline pilot. Considering his difficulties, of course, this was an unobtainable goal.

I discussed the concept of "take away, give back" with the parents and they applied this principle to their next discussion with their son. They investigated a number of airline-sponsored training programs and presented them to Scott. They told him that, although his dream of becoming an airline pilot was unobtainable, it was very possible that he could find a career working at an airport. The successful running of an airport requires the cooperative integration of thousands of professionals, ranging from cafeteria workers to baggage handlers. Without the support of these workers, the pilot's job would be impossible. Scott was advised that, although he could not be a pilot, he could be an important part of the airline industry.

When working with learning disabled young adults, the professional must also seriously consider the issue of motivation. These young people are often accused of being "lazy" or "unmotivated". Although this charge is sometimes factual, it often is the result of a misinterpretation of the person's behavior. Many times when a learning disabled young adult appears to be "lazy", he is actually suffering from "learned helplessness". This young person has experienced countless failures and defeats in his life. Many of these failures occurred in specific areas (i.e., mathematics, science, integrative tasks, athletics). As a result of these repeated failures, the person begins to develop a self-concept that prevents him from entertaining the idea of success in this area. Therefore, when asked to perform such a task, he immediately assumes that he will not succeed and, therefore, does not put forth any effort.

Everyone has areas of "learned helplessness" in their own lives. One of my areas wherein this concept impacts on my life is that of automotive repair. Despite many attempts as an adolescent to learn how to repair an engine, I was woefully unsuccessful at it. Now, some 35 years out of adolescence, I have developed in my own mind the concept that I am unable to repair an automobile and if I were to experience engine trouble, I would immediately call a garage for assistance. An onlooker may see me do this and assume that I am a lazy person because of my lack of effort to repair the car myself. I would submit that I am not a lazy person, but rather suffer from learned helplessness in this area.

In order to be an effective advocate for your child's education, you must simultaneously, come to understand your own parental reaction to the diagnosis and its ramifications.

It is widely held that parents tend to experience an unpredictable array of emotional reactions to the child and his learning problems. When parents first receive the diagnosis, they tend to DENY the problem. ("Wait 'til next year." "It will go away by itself."). This is a common and quite understandable reaction to a crisis.

Once the initial stage of Denial is finished, parents often experience a wide variety of emotional reactions that may last for days, weeks, months or even years. These stages may include:

Anger: "I hate this school." "It's not fair."

Fear: "Will she ever be independent?" "Maybe it's worse than they're telling us."

Blame: "None of this is *my* fault."

Envy: "Why do my sister's kids do so well in school and my kid doesn't? I'm a *much* better Mom than she is!"

Depression: "He's *never* going to improve."

Flight: "I'll try *anything* to 'cure' this problem."

Mourning: "He's such a good looking kid. If only it wasn't for the learning disabilities."

Going through these stages is a natural and positive process. But it is critically important to remember that Mom is often at a different "stage" than Dad and, as a result, parents may view their child's problem and performance very differently. This underscores the importance of honest, sensitive and positive communication between the parents.

It is important to remain mindful that Mom and Dad may not be simultaneously at the same stage and, therefore, are viewing the child and his situation quite differently. As a result, they find it quite difficult to communicate effectively with one another and conflict often results. As parents, you must commit to supporting *one another* as well as your child.

Transitions are, historically, quite difficult for children and youths with learning disabilities. Your child is entering a major life transition as he departs the relative "cocoon" of high school and enters the world of work or a post-secondary placement. This is not the end of a journey; it is the beginning of a new one. This extraordinary book of essays is designed to guide you on this voyage.

Lizanne Campbell's outstanding essay "Guides Along the Road" outlines her experience searching for a suitable placement for her daughter, Lara. She provides a roadmap for parents and caregivers to follow as they travel this challenging and confusing path. Her insightful article points out the profound fact that this search differs greatly from the placement process that parents experience when searching for a college placement for the "traditional learners" in their families. The process for Lara actually began in eighth grade and required a complex—but invaluable—matrix system. Among the most useful insights that Lizanne offers is the importance of the face-to-face interview and the value of preparing the candidate for this critical part of the process. Lizanne writes with the head of an entrepreneur and the heart of a Mom . . . a formidable and effective combination.

The second article "Options for Independence" was written by my great good friend and colleague, Helen Bosch. Drawing on her extensive experience with this special population of young adults, Helen offers blazing insights into the Post Secondary world and gives advice that will be invaluable to parents and professionals alike. She encourages parents to "think outside the box" as they search for post secondary placements and to develop an extensive network—consisting of friends, consultants, professionals and the Internet—to facilitate this search. As I read her article, I was struck by the number of times that she used the words "independent" and "nontraditional". Again, this is testimony to Helen's rich and varied experience in the field. She recognizes that the *goal* is always "independence" . . . and the *route* to that goal is invariably "nontraditional".

Among the most valuable parts of Helen's essay is a comprehensive list of questions to ask when exploring post secondary options. Xerox it! Laminate it! And take it with you on each and every interview. Always remember that the program is interviewing YOU . . . and YOU are interviewing the program!

Leslie Goldberg, author of "Post Secondary Options; College Isn't the Only Path After High School", is held in great esteem by her fellow

Educational consultants and is often referred to as the "Consultant to the Consultants". Her knowledge of post secondary options for non-traditional learners is immense and, because she has visited and examined most of these programs, her first hand-insights are invaluable.

Her article makes a convincing argument that college is simply not a "good fit" for every high school graduate. A secondary diploma does not guarantee that the graduate has sufficient language, cognitive or social skills to be successful in a four-year college program and many parents should examine non-traditional offerings such as apprenticeships, vocational programs and "bridge schools". She emphasizes the importance of considering the graduate's aptitude AND interests when searching for post-secondary placement.

Leslie has guided countless families on this journey. You could have no more knowledgeable or insightful guide.

In Chapter Four, Michael Pacheco provides a rich and detailed resource guide for parents and professionals as they search for placement after high school. "Non Traditional Education for People with Learning Disorders" offers an impressive directory of programs, websites and agencies that will serve as partners during your search. His "Create-A-School" checklist will be of great assistance as you attempt to identify and quantify the graduate's strengths, weaknesses, needs and interests. Michael provides you with much "food for thought" that will enable you to focus and quantify your search efforts.

Marsha Glines essay, "On Post Secondary Opportunities for Learning Disabled Students: Establishing Connections" reminds us all of the profound fact that:

"Many young adults with LD will do OK for themselves...but very few will do OK by themselves."

Marsha underscores the importance of ongoing counseling, advising and coaching for these struggling young people. "Independence" does not mean "going it alone". Rather it means the effective and timely use of our personal support systems to receive advice and counsel when it is needed. As I look at the overstuffed Rol-o-dex on my desk, I recognize that each little white card contains the name of a person in *my* support system . . . someone whom I can contact when I need counsel, comfort or camaraderie. Marsha wisely reminds us that these support systems will contribute greatly to the success of these young adults.

Chapter Six is Kathryn Zachary's provocative essay on volunteerism entitled "To Serve or Not to Serve." In an era when "community service" is misguidedly being used as a *punishment* for white collar crime, Kathryn provides a wonderful perspective on volunteerism as a mutually-beneficial process that offers the young adult with the unparalleled opportunity to "do well" and "do good" simultaneously.

Unfortunately, many special programs view "volunteer work" as a method of "filling the person's schedule" for the client who is not able to work or attend school full time . . . "It gives them something to do". Kathryn challenges this myth by outlining the important academic and social skills that can be learned via volunteer work . . . and the significant and meaningful contributions that young people with learning disabilities can make to their communities.

Massachusetts' Favorite son, John Fitzgerald Kennedy, once said, "To those to whom much has been given, much is expected." As children, these young adults were dependent upon the kindness and generosity of others. Volunteerism allows them to experience the joy of "giving back".

Ruth Antonucci's essay, "Planning Ahead: Helping Your Teen Transition from School to Work," puts a human face on the complex process of school-to-work transition. She emphasizes the importance of teamwork and collaboration in the search for appropriate post secondary employment and the establishment of an effective "match" between the young adult and the job. Her checklists and user-friendly dot-pointed text provides the reader with a complete outline of the goals, objectives and pitfalls of the job search. By following her sage counsel the parent is unlikely to place the young adult in a position that does not compliment his profile.

~ ~ ~

There are several books and media available for parents and professionals who are assisting young adults with their post-secondary plans. But I am yet to see one that is as succinct, insightful and readable as *Success in Many Shades.* I congratulate the authors and commend them for donating their efforts and talents to Learning Disabilities Worldwide. As you seek post secondary placement, you are embarking on a challenging journey. To successfully complete this trek, you will need a compass, a roadmap and survival supplies.

In *Success in Many Shades,* Lizanne, Leslie, Marsha and Kathryn provide the compass...Helen and Ruth contribute the roadmap...and Michael and Betsy offer the supplies. Bon voyage and travel safe!

With every good wish,

Richard D. Lavoie
Visiting Professor, Simmons College

Preface

A prior book, *Transitional Skills for Post Secondary Success . . . Reflections for Students with Learning Disabilities,* was intended to help students understand the transition from high school to college. Choosing the appropriate college or university is vital for students with learning disabilities. We received many phone calls thanking us for the book and suggesting we think about publishing more books to assist with this very important time of transition. I realized that students who might not be attending a traditional college also need guidance.

Regardless of their learning style or severity of disability, I believe that every individual has a destiny and a purpose to fulfill in our world. This book is geared to students who will be planning other paths for their post-secondary options. Parents and the professionals who work with them will be presented with many options by the authors. It is my hope that the ideas offered in this book will help guide parents and make a positive difference in the lives of children. The mission of Learning Disabilities Worldwide is to work to enhance the lives of individuals with learning disabilities. Our purpose is to identify and support the unrecognized strengths and capabilities of persons with learning disabilities. We strive to increase awareness and understanding of learning disabilities. We work to create a world where all persons with LD are supported in their endeavors and feel empowered to achieve their maximum potential in their academic careers, workplace, and personal development.

May you be successful in all your endeavors and in your myriad and varied contributions to our world.

Acknowledgements

Learning Disabilities Worldwide wishes to express its sincere appreciation to the Stratford Foundation, Massachusetts, and Allen Institute, Center for Innovative Learning, Connecticut for their generous grants to fund the publication of this book. Without their support, *Success In Many Shades: A Spectrum of Post-Secondary Options* would not exist.

Many thanks to our copy editors Moira Munns and Phyllis Nissen for their countless hours of proofreading and editing; thanks to Susan Mcdonald for the art design of the cover and design and layout of the book. Your hard work is appreciated, and valued.

I would like to extend my deepest appreciation to the authors who submitted their work to make this book possible. Thank you for the commitment you have made to help parents help their children.

A special thank you to the Board of Directors, Advisory Board and the International Board of Advisory of Learning Disabilities Worldwide (formerly Learning Disabilities Association of Massachusetts LDAM) for supporting children with learning disabilities. I admire each of you for your commitment and support. LDW's dedication to disseminating information so that individuals with learning disabilities are supported in their endeavors and feel empowered to achieve their maximum potential in their academic careers, workplace and personal development is truly helping children worldwide.

Chapter One

Guides Along the Road

Lizanne Campbell

Board Member of Learning Disabilities Worldwide

I am the mother of a nineteen year old daughter with severe learning disabilities who will begin a "non-traditional" college experience this fall. Lara was accepted by all four of the programs to which she applied, and will be going to the most challenging of the four. To say that I am proud is a huge understatement. Our road to this major milestone has been paved brick by brick by many hands beginning with Lara's pediatrician and followed by many dedicated teachers and therapists, a few administrators, my ex-husband, my current husband, my step-children, other family members, other "sped" families, and most importantly and heroically, by Lara herself.

We knew from a relatively early stage that Lara would not attend a traditional college program. The acceptance of this came along with accepting Lara's severe learning disabilities and moderate ADHD. It seemed very natural and part of the package. For many families, though, the realization that their son or daughter is not bound for a traditional college comes in high school, when the college search process begins. This is most likely as a result of a diagnosis of learning disabilities late in middle school or even in high school. Therefore, the family is dealing with the acceptance of the diagnosis as well as the fact that their child needs to go to a specialized post-secondary program. Coming to terms with your child's learning disability and the fact that s/he will not be going to a traditional college program is critical to your child's future. Your child will need your understanding and support in accepting the impact his learning disabilities have on his/her post-secondary options. Focusing on your child's strengths and accomplishments at this time is vital.

Before embarking upon the road to the right post-secondary option, I wish we had had a map! My hope is to provide you with such a map. This chapter is designed to educate you by sharing our post-secondary program selection process and to ease you and your child into pursuing and evaluating your options. Knowledge is an essential first step in determining what program will lead to the greatest level of independence for your son or daughter (and for yourself!).

Among parents of children for whom a traditional college program is not within reach, there seems to be hesitancy to pursue a post-secondary program that requires risk taking and a relatively high level of independence. I would suggest, however, that now, more than ever, is the time to "push your child to the edge."

Come to the Edge

Come to the edge.

We might fall.

Come to the edge.

It's too high!

Come to the edge.

And they came,

and we pushed,

And they flew.

Christopher Logue

I am, by nature, a risk taker, so I can appreciate other parents' hesitancy to pursue post-secondary programs that are a stretch for their children. However, in order for your child to reach his/her full potential, I urge you to pursue "stretch" as well as "safe" programs.

Our journey to Lara's post-secondary program actually began when she was ten years old and I was working on *That's My Child*. While attending a seminar hosted by Arlyn Roffman, Ph.D. at Lesley University's Threshold Program, I was both thrilled and relieved to discover that there were post-secondary programs designed for people like Lara! At that same conference I was reassured by other parents that independence was possible for young adults with learning disabilities who might be unable to attend a traditional college.

Our search began in earnest when Lara began high school. (I have realized that as we enter one stage, we must begin to plan for the next stage!) A high level timeline is provided below to help you navigate through the various steps.

Timeline

Freshman & Sophmore Year	1st half Junior Year	2nd half Junior Year	1st half Senior Year	2nd half Senior Year
Gather Program Information				
	Analyse Program Information			
	Narrow List to 3 - 5 Programs			
		Define Goals		
		Visit Top 3 - 5 Programs		
			Select Programs to Apply	
		Learn Application Requirements		
		Perform Psychological Evaluation		
			Submit Applications	
			2nd Visits & Interviews	
				Decide!

When Lara was in eighth grade we attended annual post-secondary fairs at her middle/high school. There we spoke with representatives from a variety of post-secondary programs. The programs ranged from community colleges and college-based alternative programs to vocational/independent living based programs. I also attended similar fairs at the Learning Disabilities Association National Conference, at a Learning Disabilities Association of Massachusetts Annual Conference, and at a local high school. These fairs are invaluable. Not only are you able to learn about the different programs, but the admissions directors can get to know your child. Also, the fairs gave Lara a glimpse of what was ahead and what her goals might be for life after high school. There is also a wealth of information at www.ldprograms.com, a website that is linked to descriptions of private post-secondary programs for young adults with learning disabilities. Your child's guidance counselor may also be helpful in locating potential post-secondary programs. Many parents with learning disabled children find working with an educational consultant to be beneficial in defining long-term goals and in searching for the right program to meet those goals.

There are two sets of goals to ponder. One is what are your child's goals for adulthood? Does he/she want to be a carpenter, a daycare teacher, a graphic designer? Is it realistic that your child will be able to live on his/her own after completing a post-secondary program, or will your child live at home or in some sort of assisted living setting? Answering these questions will help your family to define the goals of a post-secondary experience for your child. In our case, our vision for Lara is:

To live independently, most likely in an apartment shared with a friend. We believe Lara will be working full-time after a post-secondary program, perhaps in a daycare center or working for a company such as Copy Cop®. We realize that Lara will need continued assistance with money management and socialization throughout adulthood. Therefore, our goals for a post-secondary program were to:

- Deliver vocational training, positioning Lara for full-time, competitive employment after program completion;
- Assist Lara in developing her independent living skills, specifically cooking, money management, time management, apartment management, and transportation.
- Provide an environment where Lara can continue to grow socially, having a healthy and safe circle of friends, gaining confidence and competence in community and workplace settings.

Fortunately, Lara's goals and expectations were in line with those of my ex-husband, my husband, and me. You may be faced with a situation where your child has unrealistic expectations for the future. Conversations with guidance counselors as well as interest and aptitude testing may help better align goals and expectations.

We stepped up our search in the fall of Lara's junior year in high school. After attending a post-secondary fair that October, we narrowed our search to six programs. During the next twelve months we collected detailed information about each program. The resources we used to obtain information included:

- Visiting campuses (formal and 1-on-1)
- Reading web site content
- Reading program brochures
- Talking to program staff, students, and parents
- Talking to fellow parents of high school juniors and seniors
- Talking with Lara's high school staff

These resources helped us gain insight into the programs goals, structure, successes, issues, student profiles, and costs. They also helped us to assess the quality of the staff as well as their expectations for their students.

In hind-sight, we should have done one thing differently during this stage. I wish we had developed a better understanding of each program's application process sooner. We would have been better organized and probably would have gotten the applications done earlier. I did not fully understand the application requirements until late in the summer before Lara's senior year. I recommend having a thorough understanding of the application process of each of your three to five top choices before the end of your child's junior year in high school. Many of these programs, for example, have a rolling admissions policy, so applying early may be advantageous. Although many of the application requirements are similar, there are subtle differences that you need to be aware of. For example most, but not all, of the programs require something to be written by the prospective student. Some programs have affiliations with other programs and you may need to apply to the affiliate program(s) as well. Most programs require recommendations. We experienced recommendations being lost or misplaced. Be sure to keep track of whom your child sent a recommendation request to and that the recommendation makes its way to the prospective program(s).

I made a matrix to keep track of the application requirements of each of the programs we were seriously interested in. In addition to helping organize what was required by each program, I also used this to track the status of each application. (See Matrix 1)

During the spring of Lara's junior year and the fall of her senior year, we visited four programs, three of them twice. Some of these visits were one-on-one while others were more of an open house/tour style. Although Lara attended all program visits, you might be more comfortable "scouting-out" programs first. Several post-secondary programs include affiliations with other programs, such as a community college, so it is important to visit those as well. Several of Lara's friends visited programs for an overnight stay. The visits are an excellent opportunity to gain better insight into each program. You and your child will be able to see the physical setting, meet students, gain a sense of the atmosphere, and assess the talents and motivations of the staff. Be sure to meet with the program director and students; each party offers a worthwhile perspective.

Many post-secondary programs require an interview as a part of the application process. In some cases, this interview can take place during the first campus visit. In others, you may need to return for a second visit. Some of the interviews are fairly straight forward and involve meeting with one or two members of the program staff. Some programs have you and/or your child interview with up to five different staff members. Some of the interviews are done together, some with just your child, and some with just the parents. Ask in advance so that both you and your child are prepared. We also practiced with Lara, asking her questions we thought she might be asked during an interview.

Most, if not all, of these programs require a recent psychological evaluation be submitted with the application. Another lesson I learned during the application process was, never have a psychological evaluation of your child sent directly to a prospective program without reviewing it first. In our case, Lara was evaluated by someone near her residential school and, in my desire to keep the application process moving, I had the psychologist send his report directly to one of the prospective programs. The admissions director called and said, "We can't accept your daughter. She is not qualified for this program based on this report." I was devastated. When I read the report, I saw that it contained inaccuracies and portrayed Lara as lower functioning than she is. I persevered and pushed the school for a first visit. Lara impressed them. When we came back for the second visit and formal interview, she was accepted on the spot!

Many programs will let you know their decision within two weeks, with some giving you an indication at the end of the interview. Others follow the process of a traditional college program and notify all candidates at the same time (typically in the spring).

In October of Lara's senior year, I was feeling overwhelmed by all of the information, so I developed a matrix of the four programs still under consideration. This helped us compare and contrast the programs more objectively. (See Matrix 2)

After we had visited each of the "final four," Lara ranked the programs. Her number one choice was the most challenging program and the fourth program was the least challenging. She was accepted to her number three choice in November, her number one choice in December, and her number two choice in February. So we eliminated program number four in November and number three in December.

Up to this point my husband and I thought Lara's number two choice was the best program for her. Lara was persistent and articulate about why she thought number one was the right choice. "Mom, I've lived in a dorm for five years, what am I going to learn by living in a dorm for another two years? I want to live in an apartment, learn how to cook, and be independent!"

In February we were down to these two programs and not 100% sure of the right choice. So Lara and I developed a decision making matrix at my husband's suggestion. First we identified the following decision making criteria:

- Quality of staff
- Areas of study offered
- Internship options
- Opportunities for employment after graduation
- Living arrangements
- Location
- Cost

Next we ranked them in terms of importance. Then we assigned a score for each of the programs and criteria. Finally, we tallied up the scores, which were very close. The process helped us have a good discussion and I felt Lara had a better understanding of how to make a decision. Most significantly, it helped me realize that Lara was right and that the most challenging program was the best choice. Lara led me to the edge so she could fly.

Matrix 1

	Rolling	Aug. 1	Aug.1	Nov. 1	Mar. 1	Aug. 1	Mar. 1	Rolling
Deadline								
Application Form								
Parent Component	Req'd	Req'd	Req'd	Req'd		Req'd	Req'd	Req'd
Student Component	Req'd	Req'd	Req'd	Req'd		Req'd	Req'd	Req'd
High School Transcript	Req'd	Req'd	Req'd	Req'd	Req'd	Req'd	Req'd	Req'd
Educational Evaluation Results*	Req'd			Req'd	Req'd		Req'd	Req'd
WAIS-R**	Req'd			Req'd	Req'd		Req'd	Req'd
Personality Assessment***			Req'd	Req'd			Req'd	Req'd
Medical Report	Req'd		Req'd	Req'd	Req'd		Req'd	Req'd
Recommendations	3 Req'd			Req'd	Req'd	3 Req'd	3 Req'd	3 Req'd
Interview	Req'd			Req'd	Req'd	Req'd	Req'd	Req'd

*Peabody Individual Achievement Test (PIAT); or Kaufman Test of Educational Achievement (KTEA); or Woodcock Johnson, achievement section, or other comparable adult achievement test
**Wechsler Adult Intelligences Scale (WAIS). A full protocol (all sub-test scores and verbal, performance and full scale scores) is required, along with a written report.
***Full personality assessment including but not limited to the Thematic Apperception Test (TAT), Rorschach, or MMPI.
Required=req'd

Matrix 2

Program Name & Overview	Childcare	Eldercare	Culinary Arts	Hospitality	Clerical	Massage Therapy	Retail	Tuition	Room & Board	Summer Program	Total Cost
Program 1.			x		x	x	X	$27,800	$ 7,600	$ 5,215	$40,615
2-4 year program with students residing in program supplied apartments: academic/vocational courses through local community college & local business school.											
Program 2	X	X		X	X		X	$24,725	$ 9,250	$ –	$33,975
2-4 year program with students residing in dorms and 3rd/4th year(s) in own apartments with supported full-time employment.											
Program 3	X	X		X	X		X	$23,750	$ 9,000	$ 7,475	$40,225
3 year program with students residing in dorms years 1 & 2 and in program supplied apartments year 3, which includes supported part-time employment.											
Program 4	X	X		X	X	X	X	$30,100	$11,000	$ –	$41,100
1-3 year program with students residing in dorms, academic/vocational courses through local community college.											

Chapter Two

Options for Independence

Helen K. Bosch, M.S.

Executive Director, Vista Vocational and Life Skills Center
Westbrook, CT

INTRODUCTION

Watching a child graduate from high school and go on to post-secondary college life is an emotional, exciting, and anxiety-producing period for the graduate, his or her parents, and siblings. Decisions about which school to attend and what field to major in are in the forefront of the minds of the graduate and his or her family. These decisions are equally as important for the family of the young adult with learning disabilities who is finishing his or her high school experience and is preparing to move to the next step.

This next step for a young adult with learning disabilities should be filled with the same type of anticipation and excitement as it is for the typical student. The student with disabilities needs and deserves the same opportunities for leaving the family home, meeting new people, developing new friendships, and taking on the challenges of adult life. An individual's self-image as a competent young adult will depend on his ability to see himself as able to succeed without family by his side at every step of the developmental process. This concept seems so natural and filled with common sense; yet, it is often not as easy to carry out as it is to acknowledge.

Several factors combine to make these steps into adulthood bumpy for the young adult with learning disabilities. The number of options, the relative high cost of tuition and limited available financial aid, and the anxiety of the family in making this move often seem to cause the bumps in the trail to appear to be mountains. Information regarding options for post-secondary programming is not centralized, and the search for appropriate alternatives may seem daunting. However, with the right information and understanding of the continuum of programming available, the search can be productive and yield satisfying results.

The first step in this process is an emotional one. It requires families and the young adult with learning disabilities to make a clear decision that this step away from home is necessary and not just important, but essential. This sounds so simple and yet is often more difficult than is realized. Due to the nature of learning disabilities, the graduating student may not be developmentally at the same stage as the individual without learning disabilities. Often, the graduate with learning disabilities is developmentally still in his early or middle adolescence. This may lead to differences in the readiness of the family and the student to "separate" and to feel comfortable with this important transition. Sometimes, the family is ready for this move and the student is not. The student may be quite comfortable with his life and not be at all ready to upset the proverbial "apple cart." Other times, the student is anxious and eager to move away, and the family is filled with trepidation regarding his ability to succeed. It is important that the search and exploration of a post-secondary program continue even if not everyone in the family is in agreement as to whether the time is right. A good program, one that is right for the individual, will take into account the developmental readiness of the student.

The key to finding the right program is to first view this search as similar to the search for a traditional college. This search should begin about one year prior to the anticipated entrance into a program. Research available options, obtain written materials, use the Internet, get names of references, and visit as many places as seem interesting and appropriate. Include the student in the process, as he will need to feel comfortable with the choice. While the family will be very much involved, more and more decisions fall on the young adult, as he transitions away from the family home into his own community and life.

There are many options for the student with learning disabilities. The array of programs is varied both in locale and in training and technique. While many programs provide training to the young adult with learning disabilities, the style of training, living arrangements, and level of support vary from program to program. It is important to take a realistic look at the student to determine the style in which he learns best and his need for supports and structure. Individuals with learning disabilities are individuals first, and the differences among them are sometimes even more significant than those in the college-bound population.

The program components needed by the young adult should be clearly identified by the family so the search can be more objective. It will be important to analyze, through the interview process, whether the components a particular program offers match the ones the family has identified as necessary for the student's success. Of course, everyone must "feel" that the program is suitable. The more clearly defined a student's strengths, interests, and needs are prior to the visitation process, the easier evaluating the appropriateness of the program will become. This will help the family and student determine the correct match. There are many good programs, but not all are right for every person. This matching process is essential to the success and happiness of the individual as he begins this important phase of his life.

WELCOME TO A NEW WORLD—THE DIFFERENCES BETWEEN SECONDARY AND POST-SECONDARY PROGRAMMING

For families with a child who has learning disabilities, the school years have often been filled with struggle, both for the student working to make the grade, and for the family as they seek to obtain proper services for their son or daughter. Many families look forward to the post-secondary years with relief, believing that their struggle is coming to an end. Families have now entered the search for the best program for their child. In beginning this search, it is important to understand some key differences between the philosophy and role of the secondary school setting and the world of adult services. These distinct differences will have an effect on how programming is provided, and they are important to acknowledge and include when speaking to various program representatives.

Entitlement or Eligibility—A child with special needs has, by law, rights to an appropriate education that include supports that meet her educational and disability-related needs. While families often must negotiate what are necessary and appropriate services, the issue of whether the individual is entitled, within the elementary and secondary system, to receive services is usually not at question. The individual is entitled by the fact that she has a documented disability. Post-secondary programming and the adult service system are quite different. An individual with a disability will no longer be automatically entitled to an array of services or options. After graduating or aging out from her secondary school experience, the individual is now in an environment where there will be factors, or criteria, to determine if she is eligible to receive any assistance. These factors may include severity of disability, financial means, or level of perceived need.

This is an important philosophical difference between the childhood and adult systems. Families have become accustomed to the school system initiating the process for services and supports. In the adult world, the individual and her family must initiate any application for supports, funding, or programming that they may wish to receive. To further complicate this issue, programs and systems often have different criteria for eligibility. Therefore, the individual and family must research and determine the criteria for each possible service. It is essential that family members begin to work with secondary school personnel to learn about what is available after graduation in the local community as well as around the country, and how each application process differs.

Centralized or Community — As the individual is no longer automatically eligible for an array of services, an other factor to be taken into account is the decentralization of service provision. While in a school system, students identified for special education received necessary and appropriate services within the school day and integrated into the school program. While this may create its own set of issues, the coordination of services and supports was the responsibility of the school. The student was seen at the center of the circle.

In the post-secondary world, centralized services are usually no longer an option. As with college students who must seek out their classrooms and their professors, the individual and her family must seek out required special services and education. Training and support services may be community-based and in a variety of locales, with the coordination and organization of these support services left to the individual, parent, or advocate. As families explore options within their local community as well as across the country, it is important that they determine their son or daughter's ability to coordinate services.

Adult or Family — College freshmen are often struck with the sudden realization that their families are no longer there to fix problems, and that they must advocate and problem-solve for themselves. This realization is an important step into adulthood and is usually made with relative ease. The college freshman soon realizes that she is the decision-maker and that with this freedom comes a certain level of responsibility.

The same concept applies to students with learning disabilities who are entering the post-secondary world. They are viewed by all adult systems and by most adult programs as the decision-makers; yet, the individual who is developmentally delayed may not have the necessary maturity or social judgment to handle this responsibility. However, they must begin to take this responsibility or, like their college counterparts, they will never learn how to develop this skill. There is a delicate balance between providing enough freedom and responsibility and enough support and structure to ensure relative safety. Families must evaluate their son or daughter and determine realistically what level of independent decision-making they can handle. To give her no power of choice is to teach her nothing. To give her too much choice is to set her up for failure.

Families will also need to become accustomed to the concept that their input will now become secondary to the student's choices in day-to-day decisions. The young adult must play a key role in the decisions that will affect her life, as this is the only way she will develop necessary adult thinking skills.

Funding — Upon completion of high school, a free and appropriate education ends for both the college-bound graduate and for the individual who may be exploring alternative programs. The concerns about funding are two fold: programs that offer an array of special services to meet individualized needs are often quite costly, and usually very little financial aid or funding exists to offset these costs. Unless the program offers a degree and is incorporated into an accredited college, the traditional forms of scholarship and federal financial aid do not apply. Sometimes families may access state funding for individuals with disabilities to pay for certain training programs, but this is determined on an eligibility basis and each funding source has its own criteria. Families must look creatively at the criteria and advocate for their sons or daughters.

The most successful approach to funding a special or alternative program is to take a "vegetable soup" approach. No one vegetable makes a soup flavorful: the combination of several ingredients provides the richness and flavor. Likewise with funding. No one source will generally view itself as responsible for funding all aspects of a young adult's current or future services and training. Instead, families and the young adult must play an active role in seeking out funding that may be applicable. The more creative the search, the greater the possibilities. Local scholarships, state funding, federal benefits and local resources may put their contribution into the "pot." Families must also realize that they will have a responsibility to contribute, as they most likely would for a college-bound sibling.

IMPORTANT COMPONENTS OF AN ALTERNATIVE POST-SECONDARY PROGRAM

Once a family can get through the maze of funding and become accustomed to the differences between child and adult services, the next factor to consider is what the best type of program for their child would be. While every program is unique in its setting, curriculum, and mission, most institutions will include certain common features. Each potential student will require varying degrees of these components. It is important to make the right match between the needs of the young adult and the program's strengths and focus. To adequately train and provide quality services to adults with learning disabilities, programs must incorporate the following aspects into their overall mission and programming.

1. *The program must offer individualized training and services.* Each individual with a learning disability has a very different profile, level of need, and area of deficit. One individual may have difficulty processing auditory information while another may have trouble only with visually presented information. As the pervasiveness and severity of the learning disabilities increase, so does the complexity of accommodations and learning styles. While every program must have an organizational structure upon which to build, it is essential that special programs recognize the special needs of each person.

Training or accommodations may be tailor-made to the individual. The individual may receive different support services to enhance a core training or be scheduled differently depending upon her strengths and needs. It is important to evaluate the level of individualization and how it would be implemented for the potential student.

2. *Time frames should be flexible and non-traditional.* While every program will have a core length of time or range within which it operates, it is important to determine the level of flexibility in the program to allow for either greater or slower progress by the young adult. It is essential that slower progress not be seen as a failure to achieve but as part of the individual's developmental process. This should not be confused with the program's need to maintain minimum standards of productivity, which all quality institutions should have. Most institutions will provide these expectations with some degree of flexibility this assures that success is not solely dependent upon length of time nor speed of progress.

3. *Cognitive and social skills should be addressed as core components.* Individuals with learning disabilities may have trouble with social skills or social judgement as well as difficulty with organization. Social skills are the building blocks of basic relationships and "getting along" with the world. Individuals with social skill difficulties will have trouble *getting* a job, *making* friends, or *entering* the community without help. Social judgement is more complex and sophisticated and requires use of self-regulatory skills, ability to empathize, and ability to see consequences for actions. Poor social judgement is often what causes difficulty; after a person's *been on a job* for several weeks or months trouble *keeping* friends, or *ongoing* difficulty living in the community without support.

Organization is a type of cognitive skill essential to master independence. Planning, monitoring, and initiating action must occur if life is to run smoothly. If a person has even one deficit area in cognitive function, he or she will have trouble staying organized and managing daily affairs.

Social and cognitive deficits are both very common to many young adults with learning disabilities. These may be due to the disability itself, developmental delays, other associated issues, or immaturity. These deficits will most likely not be fully eradicated, yet they must be dealt with as an integral part of any program that provides training toward independence and work. Social and cognitive skills are the foundations of adult thinking necessary to living and working successfully within the community. Each program will offer a variety of techniques, but each program should be able to identify and describe how it treats these important issues.

4. *Programming should be comprehensive and address the needs of the whole individual.* Young adults transitioning to post-secondary life have generally had little experience living outside their family's home. They have relied on structure, feedback and organization provided by their parents and by living in their parents' home. They have often not learned how to disassociate one aspect of their life from another, an important adult skill. If our car breaks down, we manage to find another way to get to work. If our alarm clock fails to ring, we still manage to accomplish our responsibilities. These types of situations for the young adult with disabilities often become much larger roadblocks.

A program that addresses the life skills and emotional development of the individual must incorporate a holistic approach to training and services. A coordinated effort to assist the individual in managing all aspects of work, education, and daily life is as important as teaching him how to manage it for himself. Segmenting or separating aspects of services or training often leads to difficulty or failure, as the necessary communication and organization are not possible. Quality programming either directly or indirectly considers the entire individual from training and coordination perspectives.

Families should examine how much coordination their son or daughter requires in order to routinely function. This can be ascertained by evaluating how much of the day-to-day organization of the individual's life is currently being done by a parent or caregiver in the home. The level of oversight will be directly related to the current experience and skill of the individual.

5. *A program should recognize and address the developmental level of its student population.* Individuals with learning and other cognitive disabilities generally are delayed in their developmental growth. An individual who is 18 to 20 years old may, in fact, be functioning as a young adolescent, an issue that must be addressed for appropriate programming and training. For example, typical 18 to 20 year-olds will have the beginnings of a career identity. They will have already developed a basic work identity and now be deciding upon a career path. In contrast, 18 year-olds with significant learning disabilities may be just beginning to see work as a viable, desirable option. They may not yet have developed a work identity and are generally not ready to consider career options. To require an individual with

developmental delays to enter programming well beyond his maturity level or functioning will lead to needless failure and frustration. Programs should deal with this issue by modifying participants' expectations, creating structures and developing systems not usually seen in a traditional post-secondary environment. Programs must fit the functional and developmental needs, not the chronological expectations of their student bodies. Careful evaluation of the individual and his or her realistic functional levels in key areas such as work, independent living, and social growth is essential to finding the right match.

6. *Alternative programs should think long-term.* Families and young adults will begin to develop a picture of what they believe the next decade will entail. As this picture emerges, the chosen program should be moving in the same direction, with a similar philosophy and structure. For example, if the goal for an individual were to never work, why attend a program with a significant vocational component? Likewise, if an individual and his family believe the individual will always need a caretaker, it would be problematic to explore programming that fosters independence. It is important that not only the day-to-day services seem to be a correct fit for the individual and his needs, but that the mission and long-term goals are consistent with the attitudes and values of the family and the individual.

Each and every program around the country is as varied as its student body. Some programs offer a long-term, clearly defined program component. Other programs offer time-limited training and services designed to meet a milestone, with the expectation that the individual will move on. Each is a right match for someone. Regardless of the specific services, the program should have created services and curricula with a long-term goal and strategy for the individual.

All programs should be able to describe the belief systems and philosophical foundations that are the cornerstones of all aspects of their training. A match between the vision of the family and the philosophy of the program will lead to greater success and a sense of fulfillment for all.

BEGINNING THE SEARCH

As a family sits down with a son or daughter to begin to make decisions about the important components of a program, family members take a hard and realistic look at the individual's strengths and current and long-term needs. A picture of the preferences in programming begins to emerge. To accomplish this search, families must be open-minded about the location of the program and recognize that there might not be an appropriate program in the community near their home. Families, whenever possible, should take a national approach. While many options are available, the right match for a particular individual may be in another state or region of the country. Families can seek out information regarding options in several ways. They are:

- *Speak to local school personnel.* Special education teachers and professionals are a great resource for general information. They attend professional development conferences and seminars and collect information of interest.
- *Contact related associations.* Organizations, such as the local learning disability organizations or the special education associations, often keep files and information on available post-secondary options. While they may not deal directly with the programs, they will have enough information to get a family started. Many associations host post-secondary or related conferences in which families can meet with program representatives or hear presentations regarding options in the region or the country.
- *Contract with an educational consultant.* Educational consultants are professionals who specialize in educational planning at the secondary and post-secondary levels and help families and individuals make the right match. A family can hire a consultant to assist with and guide the search. While there is a fee, the consultants are knowledgeable and can make the search more efficient and accurate.
- *Explore the Internet.* Many programs now have websites and information on the Internet. Many also can be contacted through email and also provide phone and address information. It is important that families use the Internet searches for initial information but still obtain materials such as catalogues or brochures via regular mail. Internet information often provides an introduction. Even more can be learned by requesting a packet containing much more detailed information. The additional information may help a family determine if it is a program they would want to visit.
- *Obtain directories of post-secondary programs for young adults with special needs.* Recently, several comprehensive directories, similar to those about colleges, have been written for individuals interested in alternative post-secondary programming. This is a relatively new phenomenon and a family may have to search in order to locate the directories. Large bookstores, the local library, the disability services office of a local college or university, or the

local disability association would have copies of the book, or information on how to obtain copies.

- *Speak to other families with children who have special needs.* Word of mouth continues to be one of the best resources for families across the country. Often another family in similar circumstances will have heard of options and can give contact information or references.
- *Ask program representatives about other similar options.* Most alternative programs know of other available options and are happy to suggest those organizations that provide similar training. Most professional organizations will not speak about or make in-depth comparisons to other programs. This search is very personalized and can be done only by the family, based upon significant personal knowledge about their son or daughter and the values they hold.

CONTINUUM OF TRAINING—DIFFERENT PROGRAM MODELS

Young adults transitioning from a high school setting to a post-secondary instructional setting must think not only about program qualities and values, but also about the type of program they wish to attend. While a variety of programs offer training and support services to individuals with learning disabilities, there are distinct, yet subtle, differences among them. These differences may be the cause of success or failure, so it is important to recognize where on the continuum a young adult is and to choose a program that fits.

Even the broad categories described below are general. Once family members determine the general category they wish to explore, they should carefully evaluate specific programs within that category.

The following are general types of post-secondary programs for individuals with learning disabilities seeking an alternative to the traditional college program.

CAMPUS-BASED, DEGREE-GRANTING PROGRAMS—These programs are college programs in which all students in the program require similar support and academic services. Programs in this category generally offer an associate's degree in specific fields of study and have a full range of services built into the specialized curriculum. Most have a segregated, structured living environment with greater levels of services than what would traditionally be seen on a college campus. Students do not live in the mainstream dormitory. Classes may be integrated into the regular campus or specialized for this population. Services may include academic accommodations, tutoring and support, mentoring, and residential supports. To function within a campus setting, students must have a minimum level of academic achievement designated by the program, good study and organizational skills, and a level of general independence. Some programs require SATs, while others look at high school records and testing. Students must have a high school diploma. Entrance requirements generally include some form of intelligence and achievement testing. Students who do well in this setting can academically handle a college program, have a relatively high level of independence, want the academic life and degree, but need extra support and structure to succeed.

CAMPUS-BASED, NON-DEGREE PROGRAMS—These programs, located on a college campus, but generally not integrated into the mainstream of campus life, usually offer very specific fields of study, such as office assistant, childcare or human services assistant and provide a certificate upon successful completion. Most offer vocational experiences or internships as part of the core curriculum. In addition to the classes to achieve the certificate, classes are designed to build social skills and social judgement; life skills such as money management; and work-concept development. Students must be able to generalize information, as they will be expected to take what is learned in the classroom and transfer it into other settings. Students live on the college campus but in segregated settings. Classrooms are also segregated and may be in a separate building. Students may mingle with the regular college students, but are generally separated in most academic and social activities that generally offer a higher degree of structure than that seen on a typical college campus. Students may still experience a general level of independence within the dormitory and must be capable of handling a college campus without ongoing staff support. Students must have a high school diploma or certificate of completion for this option, which is viable for those students who would like to live within a traditional campus and yet would not be able to meet the academic and social demands of college life.

SUPPORTED-LIVING PROGRAMS WITH COLLEGE CLASSES — For some students with learning disabilities who wish to attend college and can be successful academically, campus living is not the best option. Supported living programs are designed specifically for those interested in attending college, but requiring greater structure and supports in their home to be successful. The supported living program is usually located in an apartment building or housing complex near a college campus. The college may be a four-year or two-year "community" college. Students must have a high school diploma, a good basic level of independence, and the academic strengths to handle college-level courses. During the day, the students attend college or university, and, in the evening, receive academic and life skills support at their home or apartment. Work is usually not the focus of the program and often the students will take a limited number of classes instead of a full course load. This option is ideal for an individual who wants to try college, but is not ready to handle the social demands, level of independence, and freedom associated with living on a college campus.

SHORT-TERM TRANSITION PROGRAMS—It is not uncommon to find students with learning disabilities who have completed high school, but are not yet ready to take on a more independent program. While they may have the academic potential, their level of maturity indicates that they are not yet ready to handle the freedom of the college environment. For these individuals, programs are designed to develop a foundation of basic skills so students may better handle either campus or independent living. Transition programs of this type are usually one or two years in length and bridge the gap between high school and a post-secondary experience. The individuals in transition programs have generally not had any independent living and need ongoing, highly structured support. Life skills, academics, and career exploration are key areas of focus in these programs, which help young adults explore their interests, build readiness for further independence, and evaluate the type of post-secondary program they might need. Often, transition programs associated with private secondary schools for students with learning disabilities are the perfect answer for the student unsure of the appropriate option and needing assistance in taking on the challenges of adulthood.

INDEPENDENT LIVING AND VOCATIONAL PROGRAMS—For many young adults with significant and generalized learning disabilities, a post-secondary program that focuses on academics is not the route to independence. Developmental delays and difficulty in organizational skills and social judgement create a need for a program with a great deal of structure and support, as well as direct hands-on instruction. Independent living and vocational programs are designed for the individual requiring instruction and training in life skills development and work skills. The goal is to develop specific skills in independent living and employment, so that the young adult may eventually integrate into the community and work successfully. Most of the programs combine classroom and experiential training in work and independent living as well as training to develop social and emotional competencies.

Students may live in an apartment building, housing complex, or a dormitory, with significant support in their living environment. Most programs are two to four years in length and are for the individual who needs comprehensive vocational and life skills training to master independence. Some of these programs may offer long-term supports after the individual successfully completes the program. Students generally have a significant learning disability, sometimes accompanied by other medical or psychological issues. A high school diploma is generally not required for acceptance. In fact, many students accomplish their high school transition requirements in this type of program, an excellent option for the individual who is ready to move away from the family home, has a basic level of self-care, and yet requires comprehensive training and supports to reach independence.

LONG-TERM SUPPORT PROGRAMS—This type of program is for the individual who has completed either a campus-based or independent living program and is ready to live within the community, but will need ongoing supports in order to be successful. Usually these programs are affiliated with a post-secondary instructional program; however, individuals may come from other programs. Housing is generally scattered throughout one or several communities, though a few programs have their apartments clustered in one or two buildings. Individuals usually rent or purchase housing and then purchase instructional support services such as life skills training, counseling, job placement and vocational support. Individuals have generally completed the initial post-secondary training and may have attended another program or college. Usually the individuals in this type of program need intermittent supports and instruction within their apartment or on their job. Recreation and social supports vary from program to program. For the individual who has completed his or her initial phase of a post-secondary program, but will require long-term and ongoing life skill and vocational supports, this is an ideal way to offer independent living within both a community and a structured program.

QUESTIONS TO ASK

For students, summer means relaxation, break from the effort and taxing schedule of school and a time to slow down . . . unless a child is entering his last year of high school in the fall. Then, the summer schedule is filled with the beginnings of the college search and the first discussions of life after high school. This holds true for families seeking alternative programming for their child's post-secondary experience. The family can take several steps to begin the process of self-evaluation and program exploration that will soon occur in earnest.

First, families should begin to work with their sons or daughters in creating dreams of the future. Whether these dreams are entirely realistic is not as important as the process, which allows the soon-to-be-adult to realize that he or she must begin to plan for the future. This process also allows the individual to begin to understand that his or her opinion and ideas are important in the decision-making process that lies ahead. In addition, the child should be given greater responsibility for planning aspects of daily life. For example, the young adult should carry greater responsibility for his own clothing and personal supplies. He should have a checking account and be required to use it for simple purchases. The greater the planning and organizational skills a student can bring to a post-secondary setting, the greater the chance for success.

Second, families should begin to speak with professionals and teachers who work with their child to create a picture of his functioning and developmental level. Families will have to spend some time incorporating this information into their own knowledge base so that a realistic picture of their child emerges. The clearer this picture, the greater the chance for a successful placement in a post-secondary program.

Third, the family must begin to explore funding options that may be available. Family members need to become knowledgeable about what, if any, resources can provide help, as this will be a factor in determining the direction taken in post-secondary planning. Speaking to school system personnel as well as trade organizations can provide an understanding as to what is available. Attending workshops or post-secondary conferences is also a way to gather the very important information about options.

Fourth, family members should discuss what they foresee as the long-term future for their child. What living arrangement, type of support, amount of financial resources, and anticipated access to the family are important points of discussion. While these may change as the child grows and develops his unknown potential, families want to choose a program that will match their fundamental values and beliefs. If families begin a relationship with a post-secondary school or program without the same vision, conflict and tension arise, and the child is placed in the middle. Values and expectations must be discussed with a potential school, so that everyone has a clear understanding from the beginning. Clear statements of expectations can help clarify potential differences and increase communication between the program and the family.

Finally, the family should begin to collect information through the many avenues already described. The greater the amount of information, the greater the knowledge base upon which the family can draw. In addition, the family should begin to explore and determine what components of a post-secondary program are important. Ranking them in order of importance for their son or daughter will help clarify what is essential and non-essential in a program.

The following list of questions can be used initially as a guide for this process and then later to determine the right match for the potential student. Programs are generally good, but there are significant differences that make some programs better for certain individuals than others. The following questions should be considered and discussed as a family prior to meeting with a school. Then, the same questions may be asked of the post-secondary program personnel. While there are no "correct" answers, some answers will give a picture of whether a particular program is the correct match for a specific young adult.

QUESTIONS ABOUT POST-SECONDARY PROGRAMMING

1. What type of living arrangements would be best? Does the young adult want/need dormitory living, campus, apartment, home? Should it be in an urban, suburban, or rural setting?
2. How much support does the young adult need i.e., 24-hour support, intermittent training, periodic check-in? What are the support services offered by the program? What are the rules? What is the disciplinary process? How do the supports differ during weekdays, weekends, and evenings?
3. How does the young adult learn best? Does he or she learn in a classroom, through simulated training, or through real experiences with supports?
4. Does the family want and the student plan to attend a time-limited training program (one to three years in length) or one that offers long-term supports and services?
5. Is there a counseling component? How is it offered i.e; through peer mentors, staff, outside professionals? Are there clear goals in this area for the young adult?
6. How are social skills developed? Are they taught in a classroom or in another venue? How is the teaching carried over into real life experiences?
7. What are the vocational options? How is employment addressed? How does the individual develop employment skills? How are they provided and what are the employment goals? Are there placement and subsequent support services to maintain employment?
8. What is the relationship that the program will have with the parents? To what extent does the program believe in and encourage parental involvement? How does the program help the family make this transition?
9. What is the staff/student ratio? How many staff are full time or part time? What positions do they hold, and what are their credentials?
10. What is the ultimate goal of the program for each student? How does the program plan to achieve it? Are these goals a match with

the family's? If not, what can everyone live with and what is non-negotiable?

11. What is the feel of the place? Does it have a blend of individuals that will form a good peer group for the potential student?

12. What relationship does the program have with the local community? What is the composition of the Board of Directors, if applicable? Is there community involvement?

SUMMARY

Independence, productivity, friendships, and ultimate success are what all high school graduates dream about as they complete their high school experience. A successful post-secondary experience is possible for each individual with a learning disability. Much work and effort goes into this process. With proper planning, objective decision-making, and the increased involvement of the young adult, this process can be exciting and the first step toward independence and success.

Many Shades for Success

Chapter Three

Post-Secondary Options: College Isn't the Only Path After High School

Leslie S. Goldberg, M.Ed. CEP

Consultant on Learning Disabilities, Hingham, MA

"*So where is your daughter applying to college?*" Does this question along with the ever popular talk of SATs, GPAs, and ACTs make you want to avoid bumping into your child's classmates or their parents? Should we create a new syndrome called ATC (Avoid Talking College) with symptoms of rushing to a mysterious appointment, or losing your voice? Although this sounds quite bizarre, it is not far from what many parents of students with more significant learning disabilities often feel.

Yes, but doesn't everyone *have* to go to college to be anybody? How will our child ever be independent enough to live on his own? The happy answer is that there are plenty of options for students who are not able to attend college right after high school, if at all. This chapter contains three sections:

I. **HOW AND WHEN DOES A PARENT KNOW THAT COLLEGE MAY NOT BE AN OPTION IMMEDIATELY FOLLOWING HIGH SCHOOL?**
II. **HOW DOES THE PARENT FIGURE OUT WHAT MAY WORK?**
III. **WHEN IS IT TIME TO LET GO?**

I. HOW AND WHEN DOES A PARENT KNOW THAT COLLEGE MAY NOT BE AN OPTION IMMEDIATELY FOLLOWING HIGH SCHOOL?

Parents will be noticing many clues by *middle school* or *junior high school* just by watching what classes their children take. If the student were college bound, the courses at this level of education would include some or all of the following courses:

- Algebra or pre-algebra
- Foreign language
- Introductory physical science or biology
- English courses with lots of reading and papers

By ninth grade, if not before, the student would be tracked in most major subject areas. For example, if your high school offers three or four levels of difficulty, the students most likely to go to college following high school would be in the highest level or two. Certainly, if your child is in the lowest ability level he will not be prepared to compete with other students who have been in the upper levels. Perhaps you have a child in a self-contained classroom or in a vocational program. Perhaps your child has needed an aide in mainstreamed classes. Perhaps your child is mainstreamed for most classes, but not all. How do you know?

The following are the basic requirements for most four-year colleges, or those granting the bachelor's degree. This is not including any accommodations or course waivers/substitutions:

- Four years of English
- Three or four years of math, including at the *very* least Algebra I, Geometry, and Algebra II
- Three or four years of history/social sciences
- Three years of foreign language
- Three or four years of science, including two of lab sciences
- One year of computer science or programming
- One year of visual or performing arts

If your child hasn't had this kind of preparation, but would still like to consider going to college, he can begin with community college. Community colleges offer open enrollment, which means he need not apply. Students simply sign up for courses, even one at a time, after taking placement tests to tell what level of remediation, if any, is necessary before taking this higher-level course. If remediation is indicated, then special courses are offered to the student until he can do the level of work in the class.

Does this mean he is any less a good person than the other students? Absolutely not! Think of the folks whose services are so important to us that we have to practically get on a wait list! Young adults can be plumbers, electricians, veterinary assistants, dog groomers, tailors, upholsterers, butchers, bakers, cosmetologists, barbers, security guards, exterminators, store clerks, nursing assistants, builders, cooks, mechanics, technicians for almost any industry.

Everyone cannot and should not go to college! This sounds very strange coming from an educational consultant, but the young adult must fit in *academically, socially,* and *cognitively* as well as show *signs of readiness* for college. Take your cues from your child. If he doesn't relish sitting in a class, taking notes, writing papers, maybe college is not the right choice, or at least not right now. You will save yourself the angst of those parents who push their children to go to college when they don't want to go. The kids never go to class, and all the parents' hard-earned money goes down the drain. So which is better: listening to the signals, watching for the signs and doing something else or wasting the money and having a child wracked with guilt and poor self esteem because he simply couldn't cut it? It's almost like a no-brainer to me. How many of your successful friends went to college later on or not at all?

Is the IQ score enough to tell if a student should go to college? NO! Of course if the score is below "low average," the likelihood that the student will be able to comprehend higher-level courses is slim. I have, however, been encouraging to those students who are the overachievers, always completing their homework, always self-advocating for help when something becomes difficult. These students, even with some relatively low scores, can take one or maybe two courses at a time while doing some hands-on vocational training. They do need extra support along with a very part-time schedule, so community college is appropriate in this case.

The guidance counselor and the special education professionals should also be indicating to you if your child should be considering higher education. If you are in doubt, call a meeting with these school professionals so that you understand what your child's options may be. If the student has an IEP, there should be an indication right on the ed plan about post secondary needs as well as if the child will be granted a regular high school diploma. However, do not be misled; even if the student succeeds in obtaining a regular high school diploma, and even if the professionals are stating that college might be okay for your child, it does not mean it is the right thing for right now.

I recently found a discussion on an e-list for professionals in the college admissions community about how to tell if a student is ready for college. A counselor had written in asking for suggestions about this topic and some of the responses were appropriate to discuss here, regardless of the learning difficulties in the classroom. The quotations were cut and pasted onto the member's response with no credit given, so it would be impossible to cite the authors here.[1]

- Students who routinely avoid the steps necessary to apply to college (such as registering for the SAT, requesting and filling in applications, making appointments with the guidance counselor, etc.) could be sending a message about their readiness for college. Very often they might not even realize this themselves, but may be indicating to parents without actually putting it into words that college should not be on the immediate agenda.

- One counselor commented that students most ready for college have demonstrated *curiosity* about themselves and the world around them; *independence* in trying new experiences outside their comfort zone, such as a foreign country; *service* to others unlike themselves; and finally *engagement* in activities with the school rather than going right home every day.

- Students who are ready have "kicked the procrastination habit."

- Another counselor mentioned warning signs: if the parent always answers for the student in an interview and the student possesses no interpersonal or speaking skills; if the student is choosing a major

---

1. NACA E-LIST, Responses to "How to Tell if a Student Is Ready for College," August 16, 2002.

based on the parents' decision, not his, then he most likely will not be successful in college.

II. How does the parent figure out what may work?

Now that we have "permission" for our children to take a slightly different path from most of their classmates, how do we know what is out there that may be right for our own child? Of course the most obvious answer is to seek professional help from guidance counselors, educational consultants, or those specializing in the field of learning disabilities. To do it on your own, the first step is figuring out your child's interests and strengths and then having a realistic assessment of what will be the biggest challenge as he becomes independent.

Interests and strengths are the easiest to figure out. Watch what your child does in his spare time.

- *Does he spend his time outdoors or inside?*
  This helps to focus on areas of interest. An outdoor person might like landscaping but would hardly be happy at warehouse work. On the other hand, a student who has to be coerced to take a walk would be better off as a pastry chef than a dog walker.

- *Is he a couch potato whose only recreational activity is the computer?*
  It's probably best to find a place where he can learn some social skills, but not necessarily too far removed from the computer field. Students who isolate themselves with television and computers often need help with independent living skills as well, since they are often hyperfocused on the computer as the world goes by.

- *Does she enjoy babysitting or caring for animals?*
  Students who seem to adore children and animals are a natural for working in these fields. They also might have the personalities for working with the elderly population.

- *Does he like to build and fix things?*
  If your child enjoys putting things together and taking them apart, he has more skills in this area, so seeking training in this area for a life job would be a good idea.

- *Has your child ever held a job or done volunteer work?*
  This is another indication of strong communication skills as well as the ability to be responsible even before becoming independent. It's always a good idea to have your children do any kind of volunteer or paid jobs before they leave high school. Working at a fast food restaurant might not be what would work for your child, but perhaps helping in a food pantry might suit him better.

If it doesn't work, don't be afraid to try something else.

Notice traits, strengths, and weaknesses like these and jot them down; soon a direction will emerge. Once you have the sense of a direction and the needs of your child, you can take the next step, which is zeroing in on where to go to get what he needs.

There are many different types of post-secondary programs, schools, and colleges from which to choose. The following are some of the types of choices available, and new ones crop up almost daily:

- *Bridge Programs*

  Some two- and four-year colleges offer summer or school-year programs that bridge the gap for students who are capable of going to college, but need more help with certain skills such as self-advocacy, study skills, and some remediation. Students often go to one of these before attending that particular college full-time. If for whatever reason it doesn't work, it is not as big an issue as flunking out of a regular college. These programs are also offered at some independent secondary boarding schools.

- *Postgraduate (PG) Programs*

  These are mainly meant for students who are college bound but need some extra maturity or skill building. These students have the cognitive and social abilities for college, but need more help in the academic arena. They may need to work on bringing up their SATs as well.

- *Postsecondary Programs*

  These programs may offer independent living skills, such as banking, shopping, cooking, doing laundry, socializing, learning responsibility without the parents' help. Academic courses may or may not be offered. If they are offered, they usually are in the nature of pre-college for the first year and then, if appropriate, the student may take some courses at the local community college. These students could never survive the sophistication of today's party scenes and might even be at risk if they were to try. These students are generally more naïve and sheltered and very well may already have some of the above skills but need to become more independent from their parents.

  Many parents are hesitant to consider such programs because they feel their child is more capable than many of the students in these programs. What usually happens is the students themselves go, visit, and feel more comfortable than they have ever felt in former environments. They usually beg the parents to let them stay!! There are many different kinds of programs like this and each offers something different. They vary by the cognitive abilities, social abilities, and academic abilities of their students. These are not places for students who have emotional problems, other than issues of self-esteem.

- *Programs for students with learning disabilities on college campuses*
The programs referred to here are generally not for the students matriculated at the particular college or university. Rather, they are like a self-contained classroom physically situated at a mainstream school.

These programs are usually not credit granting for college courses, but the students are socially in the thick of college life. Students who might consider these programs need to be more self-sufficient and socially adept than students considering the previously described options. Because the students are over 18, one can only advise them not to go to parties or not to break the law with drugs or alcohol, but they may have access to doing so. These programs are more often found in large cities, and that in and of itself can bring problems.

Some but not all students are prepared for these life decisions and well suited for such programs. If there are any doubts at all, this is not the place to start your child's post-high school education.

- *Specific LD College*
There is only one college in the country specifically designed for students with learning disabilities. This college is only an option for those who are cognitively, socially, and academically prepared for a four-year college. Although it is primarily a two-year college, most students who graduate go on to four-year colleges. Their goal is to offer strategies that might not have been offered or used by the student during high school.

- *Community Colleges*
Community colleges are wonderful for their open enrollment policies (no traditional college application process with essays and lots of waiting for decisions), their remedial and LD support as well as the accommodations they offer. They are wonderful for non-traditional students (older than 18 to 22) as well, who may be a bit rusty on their academic skills. They are the least expensive way to test the waters of the college world.

However, in addition to these qualities, some supports and options are not available that should be a part of post-secondary life for some students with more significant learning disabilities.

Very few community colleges offer housing, and if available, it is not separate from the rest of the population. This is asking for trouble in many cases, since these students are often vulnerable to other students' hazing or taking advantage of them. In addition to the lack of appropriate housing, there is an inconsistent staff for support, which may be overwhelming to those students who need it most.

Students who attend community college without a separate program for living and support should be both cognitively strong and socially aware. Students can be weak academically, however, since remediation is available.

For those who can do community college, even if it is one or two courses at a time, there is a wealth of job opportunities upon graduation. The American Association of Community Colleges (AACC) has identified the top 15 "hot" community college credit programs. Those from which students are hired immediately upon graduation, with salaries are:

THE TOP 15 "HOT" COMMUNITY COLLEGE CREDIT PROGRAMS[2]

1.	Registered Nursing	$32,757.01
2.	General Computer Technologies	$32,242.19
3.	Computer Networking	$38,767.94
4.	Engineering-Electric/Electronics	$29,464.29
5.	Computer Technician/Networking	$36,092.15
6.	Manufacturing Technology	$30,291.65
7.	Radiology Technology	$32,478.27
8	Digital Media	$35,409.08
9.	Computer Programming	$30,838.11
10.	General Skilled Trades	$25,598.03
11.	Law Enforcement	$27,975.27
12.	Dental Hygiene	$41,907.12
13.	Computer-Aided Design	$27,968.63
14.	Automotive	$29,305.72
15.	General Allied Health	$24,781.57

Once again, it is important to understand that these programs are not for all students. The more technical and science-based programs need higher cognitive levels, while the more hands-on programs might be fine for all students.

---

2. Edinfo 2002-05, July, 2002, Eric Clearinghouse for Community Colleges.

- *Vocational Schools*
  "Trade" schools, such as those for cosmetology or truck driving offer almost exclusively hands-on training, with little emphasis on classroom work, although there still will be reading and tests. These are often "proprietary" schools that are privately owned businesses, and one needs to be very careful about how long they have been in business and who accredits them. They are not consistently appropriate for students who may have needs for accommodations or more individualized support. Of course, the hands-on learning aspect may override the need for accommodations for some students.

- *Apprenticeships*
  The *Occupational Outlook Quarterly* calls apprenticeships "career training, credentials—and a paycheck in your pocket."[3] The latest issue is devoted to this subject, and it is a wealth of information. Most of the 850 different careers offering apprenticeships offer the unusual opportunity to earn while you learn. Although most folks think of the construction or manufacturing industries when they think of apprenticeships, there are many opportunities in other careers, from child care to pastry chef. Most of the official programs are registered with the Department of Labor or the State's Bureau of Apprenticeship, but those that are not official are not any less worthwhile. These would be similar to an internship, where a student learns by doing, with or without pay.
  Those with the highest earnings are: power distributor and dispatcher ($48,570), electrical and electronics repairer, powerhouse, substation, and relay ($48,540), ship engineer ($47,530) elevator installer and repairer ($47,380). [4]
  Some commonly apprenticed occupations expected to have the most job openings are: cook, restaurant and cafeteria, automotive service and mechanic, licensed practical and licensed vocational nurse, carpenter, police and sheriff's patrol officer, electrician, and hairdresser, hairstylist, and cosmetologist.[5]
  A job might be considered to be apprenticeable or be registered as apprenticeable if it meets all of the following criteria:
  ❑   It is clearly defined
  ❑   It is customarily learned on the job

---

3. Crosby, Olivia, *Occupational Outlook Quarterly*, Pittsburgh, PA, Volume 46, Number 2, Summer, 2002.
4. Median annual earnings, 2000, *Occupational Outlook Quarterly*, Summer, 2002, p.6.
5. Job openings projected 2000-2010, *Occupational Outlook Quarterly,* Summer, 2002, p. 7.

- ❑   It requires manual, mechanical, or technical skills
- ❑   It requires at least 2000 hours of work experience, and usually at least 144 hours of related instruction[6]

III. When is it time to let go?

Once your child has begun the process of individuating and becoming independent, even if it is in baby steps, you must begin to let go. Parents of children with more significant learning differences tend to hover and baby their children far longer than necessary or even recommended. As parents we won't be here forever, and our role is to enable our children to be as independent as possible. It is far more painful for the parent than it is for the child.

Even the more severely impaired need to have their own lives, albeit supervised in a protected environment. We can't keep doing everything for our children or they will never make it on their own. We teach them a learned helplessness by doing things for them that we perceive to be too difficult for them. It is a form of enabling, truly.

It is amazing to watch the young adult who is off to see a special needs program specifically geared to his level. The parents are terrified, and the child is timidly excited. If it is the right program, he won't want to leave, and it is then that the parents begin to see the light. Kids are actually happier surrounded by others who are most like them. Their adjustment is far easier than the parents'.

There are programs of every level to fill every need and desire for this very special population. If you are very careful, if you do your home-work, and if you visit at least once and allow your child to "try before you buy" and spend some time with the other students with whom he will be living and/or learning, he should be more than fine. Then it's time to go on a much-needed vacation alone with your spouse or close friend.

Your child will feel that this is a vote of confidence that he CAN do it on his own and will feel very empowered, whether or not he can verbal-ize this to you.

Celebrate! You have brought your child to his highest potential under your wings, and now it is time for him to use it without you. Let go!

---

6. *Occupational Outlook Quarterly*, Summer, 2002, p.4.

Chapter Four

Non-Traditional Education for People with Learning Disabilities

Michael Pacheco, Jr., M.Ed.

Director of Counseling and Community-Based Services,
Higher Education Information Center, Boston, MA

By this time you have decided that continuing your education is a must, but college isn't the right choice for you. Your attention turns to "non-traditional" options such as technical and vocational schools, proprietary schools, and community education programs. You quickly realize that like colleges and universities there are many institutions and choices to be made as well as a great deal of self-assessment to be done. So where do you begin? Your starting point should be getting yourself organized by outlining the steps you need to follow to make informed, appropriate decisions. This discussion will concentrate on helping you complete the decision-making process, identify available resources, and get accepted to a program that meets your needs.

MANY CHOICES, ONE DECISION

Self-Assessment

What is a self-assessment? A self-assessment is just what its name implies. It is a series of questions you ask yourself to determine your readiness for certain situations and the levels of your skills. Conducting a self-assessment is critical in making a good decision. The more truthful you are with yourself, the happier you will be in the career and school you choose. The following are some questions you may ask yourself as part of your self-assessment:

- How prepared am I to continue my education?
- What are my strengths?
- What are my weaknesses?
- Can I live on my own? Am I independent or dependent?

Answering these kinds of questions isn't easy for anyone. More often than not, we think of ourselves of being capable of anything we put our minds to, but in reality we are not always performing at the levels we think we are. To develop an objective self view it may help to take a step back and look at your high school performance, your scores from achievement tests, aptitude tests, etc. This is important because the way you answer the above questions will directly impact the decisions you make and, subsequently, your level of success.

How prepared am I to continue my education?

Do you feel as though you are ready to study at another level? Are you willing to adhere to the rigorous schedule of classes at the college/trade school level? Are you willing to commit to two to three hours of homework per day? These are some of the questions you can ask yourself to determine if you are indeed prepared to continue. Additionally, it is fair to say that colleges, universities and trade schools expect you to be able to perform at a particular level. They will expect you to be at class as often as possible usually limiting your absences to three per semester. They expect you to be on time. Reasonable accommodations usually don't affect class schedules. They also expect you to be able to learn independently and in large classrooms, sometimes with as many as 200 students. Your readiness for school may be determined by your answers to these questions plus your objective look at your aptitude in the areas you plan to study.

What are my strengths? What are my weaknesses?

These are very important questions, and your answers will have significant impact on the direction of your studies and the choice of institution you attend. Your strengths determine how much you are able to do for yourself and your level of comfort doing it. Your weaknesses, on the other hand, determine what services you may have to request from the school you go to. If you have trouble studying independently, the school may set up tutorial services for you. If you have issues with thought or information processing, the school may have to allow you untimed exams as well as provide you with a note taker, personal attendant, or other form of assistance such as video tapes or audio recordings of classes. At this point in the process it may be helpful to you to create a list on two halves of a piece of paper, one titled, "Strengths," the other, "Areas for Improvement." On the left-hand side of each half page you can list your characteristics under the appropriate heading. To the right of your entries for "Strengths," write down the services you presently receive and will continue to access as you continue your education, and to the right of "Areas for Improvement," list the services you feel you will need to assist you. This list will be important later on in helping you choose a school to attend.

Strengths	Present Services
Areas for Improvement	Services Needed

Can I live and work on my own? Am I independent or dependent?

As you begin to look at careers, schools, and your living situation, you need to ask yourself these questions. Your answers will point you toward certain fields of study, certain schools, and certain communities or campus situations. If you believe that you are truly capable of living on your own with minimal assistance from others, you will enjoy the greatest number of options. You'll be able to consider schools outside the area where you presently live. You will be able to look at schools with dorms. You'll be able to choose fields of study that require you to work on your own or with limited supervision and assistance. For those of you who are more dependent or require assistance from other people for activities of daily living, you still have a considerable number of options available to you. There are over 4000 institutions of higher education and training in the United States. Many of these are local institutions that don't have dorms. Many are small schools, so they don't have large classes. Many have special services or departments for assisting students with various types of disabilities. Again, the biggest factor in your success is your being honest with yourself about the answers to these questions. If you can't be honest with yourself, don't expect to be successful at your school of choice.

Desired Career

Now that you have taken a good, hard look at yourself and you're confident that you have been truthful about your strengths, weaknesses, level of independence and academic abilities, it's time to think about your future career. Why do you have to decide on a career, now? You don't, but you do need to decide upon a field or occupational area you would like to go into because you can't begin to narrow down your choices for schools or educational programs until you do. Furthermore, it is important to remember the difference between a job and career—a job is something you do for a pay check, a career is something that you do because it means something to you and you just happen to get a paycheck for doing it. You don't have to be 100% certain of a specific job title, but it helps to have a good sense of the field or area of study your career will be in. For example, you may believe that you are going to be an architect, then realize you'll have to go to school or college for at least four years after high school. But you don't want to go to school for another four years. So, what are your options? You could choose a training or certificate program to become a draftsman, computer-aided design machine operator or 3-D model designer. Whichever way you go, your choices should take into consideration your likes, dislikes, abilities, and values. In other words, the career field you plan to go into should provide you with an environment in which you will thrive, feel comfortable, and succeed.

CREATE-A-SCHOOL

Above we explored who you are and what you want to do when you grow up, right? Now, we have to figure out where you are going to get the training and education you need to do it. One of the ways you can figure out where you should go to school is to design the school that would be perfect for you, then look for one that comes the closest to that model. I call this process "Create-A-School." On the next couple of pages you have a check list of characteristics that can be found in colleges, universities and trade schools. Check the traits that you want under each category. When you are done with this, we'll go over the steps for finding the best matching school.

Type of School/Program

— Technical/vocational school
— Business school
— Proprietary school (culinary institute, beauty academy, etc.)
— Computer training school
— Public job training program
— Community college
— 2-year junior college
— 4-year private college
— 4-year public college

Type of Credential upon Completion

— Diploma
— Certificate of completion
— Certificate of training
— Associate's degree
— Bachelor's degree

Size of Student Body

— Small (up to 2,000 students)
— Medium (2,001–6,000)
— Large (6,001–12,000)
— Very large (12,000 +)

Campus Setting

— Urban (large city, 250,000+)
— Urban (small city 80,001-250,000)
— Suburban (10,001-80,000)
— Rural (10,000 or less)

Location
State(s) where school/program is located: _____

_____

Programs of Study

List the classes or major subject areas you need for the career you
want: _____

_____

_____

Activities at the School
— Chorus
— Band
— Sports
— Dance
— Drama
— Newspaper
— Other _____

Admissions Requirements
— High school diploma/GED
— No SATs or ACTs
— All applicants accepted
— Average high school grade = C or better

Availability of Financial Aid
— Eligible to administer both state and federal financial aid
  programs

Support Services/Special Programs
— Services for learning disabled students
— Tutoring services
— Student employment
— Dorms

Matching Skills with Requirements

Remember earlier we asked you to evaluate yourself, your skills, and competencies. Now is the time to really look at that information and use it in a decision-making process. Pull out the list of your strengths and make a list of requirements and prerequisites for the areas of study or training programs you are interested in attending. Compare your skills to the requirements of the programs. The more skills that match the requirements of a program, the more likely you are to experience success. Keep in mind that this is not the sole determining factor on where you choose to go to school or for training. Rather, it is a component of the overall decision-making process. You along with your parents or other supportive people in your life will need to look at the whole picture of what going to school or entering a training program entails, take all of these things into consideration, and make a choice. Other points of consideration include such things as the school's location to your supports and support systems, the availability of support services at the school, the amount of financial aid offered (if this is necessary for you to attend), and classroom size, among other things.

Location

Location of the school, aside from the availability of support services, may be the single most important factor when deciding on a school or training program. The proximity of the school to your primary support system of family, friends and significant others as well as community services will and should play a major role in your decision. Another important consideration goes back to your self-assessment of independence versus dependence. The more independent you are from family, support services, and community services, the farther away from home you can look to go for training. However, if your need for family, friends, and support services, is considerable, then you will want to restrict your choices to programs and schools in the vicinity of those things. For example, it may be necessary for you to use public transportation to get to the program. You would not want to consider programs not reasonably accessible by bus, train, trolley, etc.

Size of School

There are two primary concerns regarding the size of the school or program you are entering: the overall size of the student body and the size of the average class. These are important because you want to ensure that you receive the attention and direction necessary for your success. The chances of this happening at a large to very large institution are very slim. The larger school usually means larger classes, especially in more popular programs and general education classes. In other words, the classes you would have to take could have too many people for you to learn well. A plus to a larger institution or program may be the availability of support services to accommodate you in lieu of smaller classes. Because these services come at a considerable cost to the institution, larger, more wealthy, or better funded schools and programs are more likely to have them available.

Availability of Support Services

Schools, colleges, training organizations vary as much in the support services they have available to you as they do in their missions and the courses they offer. Therefore, if you have the need for academic support and assistance from the school, you should do your research. Are the following types of services offered at the school/program you are interested in? Even if all of them aren't offered, are those that you are most likely to use available?

- individual academic support and advising
- alternative media transcription:
  - ❐ large print
  - ❐ Braille transcription
  - ❐ audio cassette
  - ❐ computer disk
- volunteer reader services
- classroom notetakers and transcribers
- tutorial services—individual and group
- oral and sign interpreters for the hearing impaired
- classroom relocation due to inaccessibility
- *exam accommodations* where relevant
- screening and referral for learning disability assessment
- equipment loan

If you answer no to the previous questions and you feel that you cannot or will not be successful without certain services, then you should contact the schools/programs not meeting your requirements. The information you are using to make your decisions may not be up to date or services available through a specific department on campus may not be highlighted in their promotional/informational materials. If after contacting the school or program, you discover they do not have the services you need, remove the program from your list.

Availability of Financial Aid

A very real concern for most people pursuing any kind of education is how they are going to pay for it. In most cases, people apply for financial aid. In doing so, they are looking for federal, state, and local grants to help cover the costs of tuition, fees, books, transportation, etc. Not all schools, programs and organizations can process or award financial aid packages. Others cannot even accept federal or state monies because they are not accredited educational sites. This means you have to do your research and ask questions of your contact people at the schools or programs. You need to ask specifically about the availability of financial aid at the institution/organization. If you don't have the means to pay for the classes from your savings or money from your family and the responses you get from the school are anything like, "All we offer are a number of financing options," "We don't accept Pell Grants or state aid," or "The only types of financial aid that can be applied here are loans," then you really want to exclude that program or institution from your list because the financial burden is going to be solely upon you. Especially with loans or borrowed money, you need to make sure the field you are going into has a good hiring future and average salaries that will allow you to pay back your loans. Otherwise, you could be creating a considerable number of problems for yourself.

Resources for finding schools and courses

In this section, you will find a number of print-based and web-based resources that can help you in your search for various programs of study, institutions with support services, understanding and applying for financial aid and many other topics related to continuing your education. The section is annotated to give you a sense of the type of information you can get from each resource.

BOOKS

- The College Handbook, 2004, 41st Edition, The College Board, New York: College Board Publications, 2003.

  This guide lists over 3,600 two- and four-year colleges and universities in the United States. It provides information regarding financial aid, admissions, deadlines, and much more.

- *Learning How to Learn: Getting into and Surviving College When You Have a Learning Disability*, Revised Edition, Cobb, Joyanne, Child Welfare League of America, Incorporated (NBN), 2003
  A book designed to walk a person with learning disabilities through the college search and application process.

- Index of Majors and Graduate Degrees, 2004, The College Board, New York: College Board Publications, 2003.
  A companion guide to the College Handbook. This guide lists schools and institutions under the majors and study areas they provide.

- *The K&W Guide to Colleges for the Learning Disabled, 7th edition,* Kravets, Mary Beth and Wax, Imy, Princeton Review Publishing/Random House, Inc. New York, NY 1997.
  This guide provides a list of colleges that provide considerable services for students with learning disabilities.
- *Peterson's Colleges for Students With Learning Disabilities or ADD,* 7th Ed, Peterson's Guides, Lawrenceville, NJ, 2003.
  This guide provides information on 750 institutions with programs for students with learning disabilities. It also provides tips for gaining admission to college.

WEB SITES

- Adaptive and Assistive Technology, www.rehabtool.com
  Provides a variety of adaptive equipment including communication devices, computer access equipment,and cognitive rehabilitation tools adapted to the special needs of the differently abled.

- Collegeboard.com
  The College Board's web site provides parents and students alike with many opportunities for exploring colleges and scholarships.

- Council for Learning Disabilities (CLD)
  CLD provides resources for professionals in the field of learning disabilities.

- Division for Learning Disabilities (DLD)
  www.dldcec.org
  DLD is the division of the Council for Exceptional Children devoted to learning disabilities. It provides information and conferences for parents and professionals.

- ED.gov
  ED.gov is the United States Department of Education's web site. It provides a multitude of information about pursuing education and securing financial aid.

- Edinfo.org
  The web site for the Higher Education Information Center provides students and their families a multitude of information for continuing education in a variety of settings.

- Finaid.org
  This is a web site that will help you find everything you need to know about financing your education.

- The International Dyslexia Association (IDA)
  www.interdys.org
  The IDA facilitates training in language programs and makes available publications relating to dyslexia.

- Learning Disabilities Association of America (LDAA)
  www.ldanatl.org
  LDAA, a national organization, that works to find solutions for a broad spectrum of learning problems. It provides fact sheets, publications, bulletins, and other resources.

- Learning Disabilities Association of Canada (LDAC)
  www.ldac-taac.ca
  LDAC publishes books and pamphlets that may be useful to U.S. residents.

- LD Online
  www.ldonline.org
  LD Online is a web site that provides parents and professionals with information and resources about learning disabilities.

- LDResources.com
  This site is dedicated to pointing parents, families and people with learning disabilities in the direction of resources online, in the community, and in the library.

- Massachusetts Rehabilitation Commission LD/ADHD Task Force, http://www.state.ma.us/mrc/ld/ld.htm
  The site provides information about the Task Force, its mission, its goals and lists a number of resources available to persons with LD/ADHD and their families.

- National Adult Literacy and Learning Disabilities Center (NALLDC)
  www.nifl.gov/nalldtop.htm
  NALLDC offers free publications, training, and technical assistance to professionals working in the fields of adult literacy and learning disabilities.

- National Center for Learning Disabilities (NCLD)
  www.ncld.org
  The NCLD offers a variety of services including referral services, education, outreach, and legislative advocacy.

- Recording for the Blind and Dyslexic (RFBD)
  www.rfbd.org
  RFBD provides over 75,000 books in electronic format, as well as other products that help people to read.

- University of Connecticut - A.J. Pappanikou Center for
  Developmental Disabilities,
  www.uconnced.org
  *The Pappanikou Center provides a number of resources for people with
  learning disabilities including an assistive technology lab that conducts
  conferences, reviews software, and publishes the ConnSENSE Bulletin.*

- Take-A-Class.com
  *This web site allows you to look up classes in your area by entering key-
  words. It also provides you with basic information about the school
  offering the program.*

Next Steps

By now, you must be feeling pretty proud of yourself. You have
accomplished quite a bit. You have taken a very close look at yourself,
your skills, your areas for improvement, your level of independence and
more. You have come up with quite a picture of yourself and the things
you need to be successful. You've taken this information and used it to
help you decide on a career area or field of study. You've also used it to
help you put together a list of possible schools or programs to apply to.
Now, you are at the point where the rubber meets the road, the point
when you decide on the programs you are going to apply to. Using
resources such as those mentioned earlier along with your in-depth self-
assessment and the profile of a school you created, you will narrow
down your choices to a list of four or five possibilities. Of the four or five
choices, one or two will be a school(s) or training program(s) you have
always dreamed of completing, two will be programs you would be
happy to be accepted into, and one will be a program to which you will
be virtually guaranteed admission. For many people this last
school/program choice is their local community college because of its
open admissions policies, the availability of financial aid, and the offering of both certificate and degree programs.

Making the Choice, Weighing the Options

You've put together your list and are faced with the task of narrowing
it down. You want to make sure the programs you apply to are good
choices. You've researched the availability of services, taken into account
your living situation and how the environment compliments your learning style. Now you want to ask yourself some final questions that will
cinch your list. Am I looking for just job training? Am I looking to get
into the workforce quickly, but would like to get a college degree in the
future? Am I interested in being marketable for a particular field regard-

less of job title? These three questions will help you narrow down your choice by helping you determine the type of institution or program you should apply to. For instance, if you believe that all you want is job training, then the types of programs you are going to look for may be opportunities through your local Workforce Investment Act (WIA) One-Stop Center. The One Stop-Center will have information on various short-term training programs in your area. It will also be able to provide you with in-depth career counseling, job seeking support, and job readiness skills. Other resources for this type of training and information are the trade unions and local proprietary schools. The trade unions may list local employers that provide on-the-job training opportunities. They can also provide you with information regarding the types of specific jobs available in the area and the average salaries. Proprietary schools do exactly what their name denotes. They charge you to learn a specific trade. The most common are commercial driving, business, secretarial, and beauty schools. These schools frequently offer short-term, intensive classes designed to teach the basic skills you need to perform a certain kind of job. This often comes with a sizeable price tag.

Although community college and four-year colleges are usually classified as "traditional" learning environments, many offer what may be classified as "non-traditional" training opportunities. Many offer one year or shorter programs that train a person to enter the workforce relatively quickly. These programs are generally offered through the institutions' Division of Continuing Studies. These types of programs are good for people who want to get into the workforce quickly, but see a college degree in their future. Why? Because the courses, although through the division of continuing education, are offered by the college and carry college credits. The credits may be applied to a college degree in the future. Additionally, community colleges usually accept and award all types of financial aid, so if this is the only way you can afford to continue your studies, community college may be your option. Furthermore, the community colleges often have the best support services and systems for people with all types of disabilities.

For the person whose primary goal is to enter a particular field, not a particular job, and for whom college credits are not important, viable options may consist of computer training schools, radiology schools, medical assistant training programs, etc. These kinds of programs usually provide the student with a general education in the field allowing them to perform a number of different duties within a variety of settings. These programs can be offered by proprietary schools, community colleges, four-year colleges, private training schools, technical institutes, and the adult-learning divisions of many vocational-technical high schools. Some of these schools take financial aid, some don't. Some have extensive prerequisites for their programs, others don't. For those looking into these kinds of courses it is very important to ask the types of questions mentioned earlier to be certain that you don't find yourself in a regrettable situation.

Now you know the three major directions you can go in, and you have chosen a particular path. Your list contains the names of four or five programs you'd be happy to attend. The next step is calling these schools for all their application materials and procedures. Some schools require that you work with a particular person in their organization to complete the application process, others expect you to do it on your own. For those who have to do it for themselves, check to see if there is an Educational Opportunity Center or College Access Center in your community to help you through. These organizations are usually listed in the yellow pages of your local phone directory. Once the admissions application materials are completed, you have to do the same for financial aid or educational financing. The two most important things to remember while going through these processes are 1) meet every deadline-DON'T TURN ANYTHING IN LATE and 2) CHECK EVERYTHING TWICE-THEN HAVE SOMEONE ELSE CHECK IT TWICE- NO MISTAKES. If you keep these two things in mind, the application processes will run much more smoothly for you.

As I am sure you have recognized by now, the decision to continue your education, whether you're going to college or into a non-traditional program, takes a lot of planning and consideration. But, by following the steps outlined, you will be able to put together a list of schools/programs, apply to them, attend one, and graduate. Good luck in your educational endeavors, and remember there are people to help you if you only ask.

EDUCATIONAL DIRECTORIES AND REFERENCE GUIDES AVAILABLE AT THE HIGHER EDUCATION INFORMATION CENTER

Please note: This bibliography is in the process of being updated. Newer titles are listed in italics. (June 2002)

1995-96 Accredited Institutions of Postsecondary Education, American Council on Education, Washington, DC, 1996. *(Available through Oryx Press, Phoenix, AZ).*

The Admissions Essay, Power, Helen and DiAntonio, Robert Lyle Stuart Books/Kensington Publishing Group, New York, 1998.

The Adult Student's Guide, 2nd edition, Grossman, Leigh and McBain, Lesley Swordsmith Books, Pomfret, CT, 2001.

African-American Student's Guide to College, Parham, Marisa and Manie Barron, Princeton Review Publishing/Random House, New York, NY, 1999.

America's Best Colleges: 1998, U.S. News and World Report, Inc., Washington, DC, 1996.

America's Best Graduate Schools—Year 2000 Guide, U.S. News and World Report, Inc., Washington, DC, 1999.

America's Lowest Cost Colleges, Roes, Nicholas, NAR Publications/Lifetime Books, Inc, Hollywood, FL, 1997.

The Art Student's College Guide, Sweetow, Linda and Brown, Carol, Macmillan, New York, NY, 1996.

Back to School: A College Guide for Adults, Ludden, Laverne L., Park Avenue Productions, Indianapolis, IN, 1996.

Barron's Best Buys in College Education, Solorzano, Lucia, Barron's Educational Series, Inc, Hauppauge, NY, 1998.

Barron's Guide to Graduate Business Schools, 11th edition, Miller, Eugene, Barron's Educational Series, Inc., Hauppauge, New York, 1999.

Barron's Guide to Medical and Dental Schools, 9th edition, Wischnitzer, Saul, Barron's Educational Series, Inc., Hauppauge, New York, 2000.

Barron's Profiles of American Colleges, 22nd edition, Barron's Educational Series, Hauppauge, NY, 1998.

Barron's Top 50: An Inside Look at America's Best Colleges, Fischgrund, Tom, ed., Barron's Educational Series, Inc., Hauppauge, NY, 1995.

Bears' Guide to Earning Degrees by Distance Learning, 14th edition, Bear, John and Bear, Mariah, Ten Speed Press, Berkeley, CA, 2001.

The Best 331 Colleges, 2001 edition, Franek, Robert, The Princeton Review, Random House, Inc., New York, NY, 2000.

Black Excel African American Student's College Guide. Black, Isaac. John Wiley and Sons, Inc., New York, 2000.

The Black Student's Guide to Colleges, 4th edition, Beckham, Barry, Madison Books, Lanham, MD, 1997.

Bricker's International Directory of University-Based Executive Programs, 1996, 27th edition, Peterson's, Lawrenceville, NJ, 1996.

Chronicle Four-Year College Databook 1998-99, Chronicle Guidance Publications, Inc., Moravia, NY, 1998.

Chronicle Two-Year College Databook 1998-99, Chronicle Guidance Publications, Inc., Moravia, NY, 1998.

Chronicle Vocational School Manual 1998-99, Chronicle Guidance Publications, Inc., Moravia, NY, 1998.

College Applications and Essays, Van Raalte, Susan D., Macmillan General Reference, New York, NY, 1993.

The College Application Essay, McGinty, Sarah Myers, College Board Publications, New York, NY, 1997.

College Credit Without Classes: How to obtain academic credit for what you already know, Carroll, James L., Central Michigan University, J.G. Ferguson Publishing Co. IL, 1996.

College Guide for Parents, 3rd edition, Shields, Charles J., College Board Publications, New York, NY, 1995.

The College Board Guide to 150 Popular College Majors, College Entrance Examination Board, New York, 1992.

The College Handbook, 2002, 39th edition, College Entrance Examination Board, College Board Publications, New York, 2001.

The College Handbook for Transfer Students, 1996, College Entrance Examination Board, College Board Publications, New York, NY, 1995.

College Online, Duffy, James P., John Wiley & Sons, Inc, New York, NY, 1997.

College Transfer Guide, School Guide Publications, New Rochelle, NY, 1997.

Colleges with Programs for Students with Learning Disabilities or Attention Deficit Disorders, 6th edition, Mangrum, Charles T. and Strichart, Stephen S., Eds., Peterson's, Lawrenceville, NJ, 2000.

Complete Book of Colleges, Princeton Review Publishing/Random House, Inc, New York, NY, 1999.

The Complete Medical School Preparation and Admissions Guide, 3rd edition, Goliszek, Andrew, Healthnet Press, Winston-Salem, NC, 2000.

Directory of Accredited Institutions, 1999, Accrediting Council for Independent Colleges and Schools, Washington, DC, 1999. (in binder)

Directory of Career Training Schools, 1997-98, Massachusetts Association of Private Career Schools, Lexington, MA, 1997.

1997-1998 Directory of Private Career Schools and Colleges of Technology, Accrediting Commission of Career Schools and Colleges of Technology, Washington, DC, 1997.

Directory of Resources for International Cultural and Educational Exchanges, United States Information Agency, Washington, DC, 1996.

The Directory of Vocational & Training Schools in Massachusetts, Experience Unlimited/Freelancers Over Fifty Foundation, Cambridge, MA, 1997.

The Educational Register: 1997-1998, Vincent/Curtis, Boston, MA, 1997.

Facts 1999: The Directory of New England Colleges, Universities and Institutes, New England Board of Higher Education, Boston, MA, 1999.

The Fiske Guide to Colleges 2002, Fiske, Edward B., Sourcebooks, Inc., Naperville, IL, 2001.

GED en Español, 5th edition, Serrán-Pagán, Ginés et. al., Macmillan General Reference, New York, NY, 1996.

Getting a College Degree Fast: Testing Out & Other Accredited Short Cuts, Aber, Joanne, Prometheus Books, Amherst, NY, 1996.

The Gourman Report: A Rating of Graduate and Professional Programs in American and International Universities, 8th edition, revised, Gourman, Jack, National Education Standards, Random House, Inc., Los Angeles, 1997.

The Gourman Report: A Rating of Undergraduate Programs in American and International Universities, 10th edition, revised, Gourman, Jack, Princeton Review Publishing, Los Angeles, CA, 1997.

Graduate Admissions Essays, Asher, Donald, Ten Speed Press, Berkeley, CA, 2000.

Gruber's Complete Preparation for the New SAT, Gruber, Gary R., Ph.D., HarperCollins, New York, NY 1993.

Guide to American Graduate Schools, 8th edition, Doughty, Harold R., Penguin Books, New York, NY, 1997.

A Guide to College Programs in Culinary Arts, Hospitality, and Tourism, 6th edition, International Council on Hotel, Restaurant and Institutional Education, John Wiley and Sons, Inc., New York, NY, 1999.

A Guide to Cooking Schools, 1996, 8th edition, Shaw Guides, Inc., New York, NY, 1995.

Guide to High Schools, College Board Publications, New York, NY, 1994.

Health Professions Education Directory, 27th edition, American Medical Association, Chicago, IL, 1999.

Help Yourself – Advice for College-Bound Students With Learning Disabilities, Princeton Review Publishing/Random House Inc, New York, NY, 1996.

Historically Black Colleges and Universities, Macmillan, New York, NY, 1995.

How to Choose a Career & Graduate School, 1999 edition, Newsweek, Inc. and Kaplan Educational Centers, New York, NY, 1998.

How to Get Into College, Newsweek, Inc. and Kaplan Educational Centers, New York, NY, 1997.

How to Get Into Graduate School, 1998 edition, Newsweek, Inc. and Kaplan Educational Centers, New York, NY, 1997.

How to Prepare for the High School Equivalency Examination, Barron's, Hauppauge, New York, 1995.

How to Write a Winning College Application Essay, Revised 4th edition Mason, Michael James, Prima Publishing, Roseville, CA, 2000.

The Independent Study Catalog: A Guide to Over 10,000 Correspondence Courses, a Peterson's publication for the National University Continuing Education Association, Peterson's, Lawrenceville, NJ, 1995.

Index of Majors and Graduate Degrees, 2002, College Entrance Examination Board, College Board Publications, New York, 2001.

Inside College, Moses, Henry, College Board Publications, New York, NY, 1995.

The Insider's Guide to the Colleges, 27th edition, Compiled by Yale Daily News, St. Martin's Griffin Press, New York, 2000.

The Insider's Guide to Graduate Programs in Education, Drozdowski, Mark J. and Cullen, Patrick, Allyn and Bacon, Boston, MA, 1997.

International Student Handbook, 2002, 15th edition, College Entrance Examination Board, College Board Publications, New York, 2001.

The International Student's Guide to Going to College in America, Dalby, Sidonia, Rubenstone, Sally, and Weir, Emily Harrison, Macmillan General Reference, New York, NY, 1996.

International Students' Guide to the U.S.A., Jacobs, Ian and Shatswell, Ellen, The Princeton Review, Publishing/Random House, Inc., New York, NY 1996.

Internet Guide for College-Bound Students, Hartman, Kenneth E., College Board Publications, New York, NY, 1996.

The K&W Guide to Colleges for the Learning Disabled, Kravets, Mary Beth and Wax, Imy, Princeton Review Publishing/Random House, Inc. New York, NY 1997.

Looking Beyond the Ivy League – Finding the College That's Right for You, Pope, Loren, Penguin Books, New York, NY, 1995.

Lovejoy's College Guide, 24th Ed., Straughn, Charles T. and Barbarasue Lovejoy Straughn, Macmillan Inc. USA, New York, NY 1997.

Luddens' Adult Guide to Colleges and Universities, Ludden, LaVerne L. and Ludden, Marsha, Park Avenue Productions, Indianapolis, IN 1997.

Making a Difference College Guide, Princeton Review Publishing/Random House, New York, NY, 1996.

The Multicultural Student's Guide to Colleges, Mitchell, Robert, The Noonday Press, New York, NY, 1996.

The Official Guide to SAT II: Subject Tests, College Board Publications, New York, 1994.

The Official Guide to U.S. Law Schools 1997, Law School Admissions Council, Law Services Publications, Newtown, PA, 1996.

The Official Study Guide for the CLEP Examinations, College Board Publications, New York, NY, 1995.

The 100 Best Colleges for African Americans, Wilson, Erlene B., Plume Books, New York, NY, 1998.

Peterson's College and University Almanac, Peterson's, Lawrenceville, NJ, 1998.

Peterson's Competitive Colleges, 1998-99, Peterson's Guides, Inc., Lawrenceville, NJ, 1998.

Peterson's Culinary Schools, Peterson's Guides, Inc., Lawrenceville, NJ, 1998.

Peterson's Graduate Programs in the Biological Sciences 1998, Peterson's Guides, Inc., Lawrenceville, NJ, 1997.

Peterson's Graduate Programs in Business, Education, Health, Law and Social Work 1998, Peterson's Guides, Inc., Lawrenceville, NJ, 1997.

Peterson's Graduate Programs in the Engineering and Applied Sciences 1998, Peterson's Guides, Inc., Lawrenceville, NJ, 1997.

Peterson's Graduate Programs in the Physical Sciences, Mathematics, Agricultural Sciences, the Environment, and Natural Resources 1998, Peterson's Guides, Inc., Lawrenceville, NJ, 1997.

Peterson's Guide to Colleges for Careers in Allied Health, Peterson's, Lawrenceville, NJ, 1996.

Peterson's Guide to Colleges for Careers in Business, Peterson's, Lawrenceville, NJ., 1996.

Peterson's Guide to Colleges for Careers in Computing, Peterson's, Lawrenceville, NJ., 1996.

Peterson's Guide to Colleges for Careers in Teaching, Peterson's, Lawrenceville, NJ., 1996.

Peterson's Guide to Four-Year Colleges 1999, 29th edition, Peterson's, Lawrenceville, NJ, 1998.

Peterson's Nursing Programs, 6th edition, Peterson's, Lawrenceville, NJ, 2000.

Peterson's Guide to Two-Year Colleges, 1998, 27th edition, Peterson's Guides, Inc., Lawrenceville, NJ, 1996.

Peterson's Private Secondary Schools 1995-96, 16th edition, Peterson's Guides, Inc., Lawrenceville, NJ, 1995.

Peterson's Professional Degree Programs in the Visual and Performing Arts, Peterson's, Lawrenceville, NJ, 2000.

Peterson's Study Abroad 1999, Peterson's, Lawrenceville, NJ, 1999.

Peterson's Vocational and Technical Schools and Programs East, 4th edition, Peterson's, Lawrenceville, NJ, 1999.

Peterson's Vocational and Technical Schools and Programs West, 4th edition, Peterson's, Lawrenceville, NJ, 1999.

Peterson's U.S. & Canadian Medical Schools, 1997, Peterson's, Lawrenceville, NJ, 1997.

Police Exam Preparation Book: Guaranteed Methods to Score 80-100%, Hall, Norman, Bob Adams, Inc., Holbrook, MA, 1994.

Postal Exam Preparation Booklet, Hall, Norman, Bob Adams, Inc., Holbrook, MA, 1994.

The Princeton Review's Student Advantage Guide to The Best Law Schools, 1997 edition, Van Tuyl, Ian, Villard Books, New York, NY, 1996.

The Princeton Review's Student Advantage Guide to The Best Medical Schools, 1997 edition, Nagy, Andrea, Random House, Inc, New York, NY, 1996.

Raphael's Guide, Career Training in One Year or Less in Massachusetts, 1995-1996, The Vocational Training Research Institute of America, Needham Heights, MA, 1995.

Rugg's Recommendations on the Colleges, 19th edition, Rugg, Frederick E., Rugg's Recommendations, Fallbrook, CA, 2002.

Schools of Nursing Directory 2000-2002: Massachusetts and Rhode Island, Nursing Education Recruitment Organization Council of the Massachusetts and Rhode Island League for Nursing, Charlestown, MA, 1999.

The Student's Guide to the Best Study Abroad Programs, Tannen, Greg and Winkler, Charley, Pocket Books, New York, NY, 1996.

Study Abroad: A Guide to Semester and Year Abroad Academic Programs, Peterson's, Lawrenceville, NJ, 1999.

Surviving the First Year of College–Myth vs. Reality, Gladis, Steve, HRD Press, Amherst, MA, 1999.

Test Preparation PSAT/NMSQT and SAT I, College Entrance Examination Board, 1994.

Tips for College Success, A notebook of information compiled by the Higher Education Information Center.

Up Your Score: The Underground Guide to the SAT, Berger, Larry, et. al., Workman Publishing, New York, NY, 1996.

Virtual College, Dixon, Pam, Peterson's, Inc., Lawrenceville, NJ, 1996.

Women's Colleges, Adler, Joe Anne, and Friedman, Jennifer Adler, Prentice Hall General Reference, New York, NY, 1994.

The Young Woman's Guide to the Top Colleges, Mitchell, Robert with Majdi, Afarin, Daniel, Susan, Straus, Tamara and Ginsburg, Ann, John Wiley & Sons, Inc., New York, NY, 1998.

Your College Application, Gelband, Scott, and Kubale, Catherine, and Schorr, Eric, College Entrance Examination Board, New York, NY, 1991.

You're Gonna Love This College Guide. Nemko, Marty, Barron's, Hauppauge, NY, 1999.

Prepared by
> The Higher Education Information Center
> 700 Boylston Street, Boston, MA 02116
> (617) 536-0200 revised: 6/2002

SELECTED VOCATIONAL AND TECHNICAL SCHOOLS

This list was compiled from information provided in the *Boston Business Journal* and the Massachusetts Association of Vocational Administrators' *Directory of Job Training Opportunities for Adults.* A more comprehensive directory of area vocational-technical schools and programs, *Educational Opportunities of Greater Boston for Adults,* is published by The Higher Education Information Center in association with The Education Resources Institute (TERI). Other regions may have similar resources and directories

American Red Cross of Mass. Bay
285 Columbus Avenue
Boston, MA 02116
(617) 375-0700

Assabet Valley Regional Vocational School
215 Fitchburg Street
Marlborough, MA 01752-1288
(508) 485-9430

Attleboro Comprehensive High School
100 Rathbun Willard Drive
Attleboro, MA 02703
(508) 222-5150

Barbizon School
607 Boylston Street
Boston, MA 02116
(617) 266-6980
Program in Modeling only.

Bay Path Voc. Tech. High School
57 Old Muggett Hill Road
Charlton, MA 01507
(508) 248-6655

Bay State School of Appliances
225 Turnpike Street
Canton, MA 02021
(617) 828-3434

Blackstone Valley Regional Voc. Tech. High School
Pleasant Street
Upton. MA 01568
(508) 529-7758

Blaine! The Beauty Career School
510 Commonwealth Avenue
Boston, MA 02215
(800) 562-5464

Blue Hills Regional Voc. Tech. School
800 Randolph Street
Canton, MA 02021
(617) 828-5803

Boston Technical Center
22 Drydock Avenue
Boston, MA 02210
(617) 482-7787

Burdett School
745 Boylston Street
Boston, MA 02116
(617) 859-1900

Cambridge School of Culinary Arts
2020 Massachusetts Avenue
Cambridge, MA 02140
(617) 354-3836

Cape Cod Regional Voc. Tech. School
351 Pleasant Lake Avenue
Harwich, MA 02645
(508) 432-4500

Catherine E. Hinds Institute of Esthetics
65 Riverside Avenue
Medford, MA 02155
(617) 391-3733

Chicopee Comprehensive High School

Vocational Division
Windsor Street
Chicopee, MA 01020
(413) 594-3555

Computer Learning Center
5 Middlesex Avenue
Somerville, MA 02145
(617) 776-3500

Diman Regional Voc. Tech. High School
251 Stonehaven Road
Fall River, MA 02723
(508) 678-2891

Essex Agricultural and Technical Inst.
562 Maple Street, Box 562
Hathorne, MA 01937
(508) 774-0050

John R. Powers Modeling and Career
School
9 Newbury Street
Boston, MA 02116
(617) 267-8781

Katherine Gibbs School
126 Newbury Street
Boston, MA 02116
(617) 578-7100

Keefe Regional Technical School
750 Winter Street
Framingham, MA 01702
(508) 879-5400

LaNewton School of Beauty Culture, Inc.
636 Warren Street
Dorchester, MA 02121
(617) 427-6886

Minuteman Science-Technology High
758 Marrett Road
Lexington, MA 02173
(617) 861-6500

Montachusett Regional Voc. Tech. School
1050 Westminster Street, Route 2A
Fitchburg, MA 01420
(508) 345-9200

Nashoba Valley Technical School
100 Littleton Road
Westford, MA 01886
(508) 692-4711

New England School of Photography
537 Commonwealth Avenue
Boston, MA 02215
(617) 437-1868

North Bennet Street School
39 North Bennet Street
Boston, MA 02113
(617) 227-0155

North Shore Regional Voc. Tech. School
30 Log Bridge Road
Middleton, MA 01949
(508) 762-0001

Northeast College of Communications
142 Berkeley Street
Boston, MA 02116
(617) 354-3836

Northeast Institute of Industrial
Technology
41 Phillips Street
Boston, MA 02114
(617) 523-2813

Northern Berkshire Voc. Tech. School
Hodges Cross Road
North Adams, MA 01247
(413) 663-5383

Old Colony Voc. Tech. School
476 North Avenue
Rochester, MA 02770
(508) 763-8011

Pathfinder Regional Voc. Tech. School
239 Sykes Street
Palmer, MA 01069
(413) 283-9701

Pittsfield Vocational School
P.O. Box 1187
Pittsfield, MA 01201
(413) 448-9601

Quincy Center for Technical Education
107 Woodward Avenue
Quincy, MA 02169
(617) 984-8731

RETS Technical Center
965 Commonwealth Avenue
Boston, MA 02215
(617) 783-1197

The Rindge School of Technical Arts
459 Broadway
Cambridge, MA 02138
(617) 349-6751

The School of Fashion Design
136 Newbury Street
Boston, MA 02116
(617) 536-9343

Shawsheen Valley Regional Voc. Tech.
100 Cook Street
Billerica, MA 01821
(508) 667-2111

Silver Lake Regional Technical School
260 Pembroke Street
Kingston, MA 02364
(617) 585-3844

Smith Vocational and Agricultural School
80 Locust Street
Northampton, MA 01060
(413) 586-6970, ext. 415

South Shore Regional Voc. Tech. School
476 Webster Street
Hanover, MA 02339
(617) 878-8822

Southeastern Technical Institute
250 Foundry Street
South Easton, MA 02375
(508) 238-1860

TAD Technical Institute
45 Spruce Street
Chelsea, MA 02150
(617) 889-3600

Travel Education Center
100 Cambridge Park Drive
Cambridge, MA 02140
(617) 547-7750

Travel School of America
1047 Commonwealth Avenue
Boston, MA 02215
(617) 787-1214

Tri-County Regional Voc. Tech. School
147 Pond Street
Franklin, MA 02038
(508) 528-5400

Upper Cape Cod Regional Voc. Tech. School
220 Sandwich Road
Bourne, MA 02532
(508) 759-7711

William J. Dean Technical School
1045 Main Street
Holyoke, MA 01040
(413) 534-2071

Worcester Technical Institute
251 Belmont Street
Worcester, MA 01605
(508) 799-1945

Worcester Vocational High School
2 Grove Street
Worcester, MA 01608
(508) 799-1980

Higher Education Information Center
Prepared by the At the Boston Public Library
666 Boylston Street, Boston, MA 02116
(617) 536-0200
revised: 9/96

Chapter Five

On Post-Secondary Opportunities for Learning Disabled Students: Establishing Connections

Marsha A. Glines, Ph.D.

V.P. for Global Educational Opportunities, Lynn University

Many of our children are confused at 18. They feel vulnerable. Many do not see the whole picture or gestalt of where they are headed, or what their futures may hold, or how they are to navigate their journeys into the future. Many do not have a world view and even more lack any sense of a life plan. More specifically, as incoming college freshmen, many question "why" to their enrollment in English skills or humanities courses or advanced math classes. They do not understand the relevance of critical thinking and academic "stretching" to their lives. They often don't consider the potential of discovery, or inquiry-based thinking, of the epiphanies that come from the moment a new understanding emerges. Instead, they may struggle with the discipline of sitting through hour-long classes, liberal arts courses, in which they see no point. Perhaps they are not developmentally ready or prepared for a college campus experience.

For students in post-secondary transition, change and apprehension go hand in hand. They are exposed to new learning environments, expanded libraries, multiple computer labs, and new teachers or faculty. Research tells us that students must develop a sense of belonging to feel comfortable, accepted, and a part of the new culture that surrounds them. A sense of belonging is established by making connections. If these connections to the university or other post-secondary placement don't happen, students feel disoriented, alone, and they may isolate. They may self-medicate, binge drink, or get high. This is certainly not true of all students, but it is for many. It is these students who become at-risk, whom we lose from post-secondary placements. Sometimes our learning disabled students who head to college at 18 and who are confused about how to make all their learning and all their experiences relevant to their immediate lives are at-risk. They have left behind the comfort of a "known neighborhood" and corresponding schools and now must share their living space with new faces and new personalities; they must learn to navigate the new "neighborhood," away from their families. While home may not have been perfect, it was predictable and offered support: parents provide a variety of structures. Now faced with new decisions, unsupervised free time, and removed from accountability, our young folks search and experiment. So many choices.

Many 18-year-olds continue to appear and behave very developmentally young. They are so often conflicted and struggle. Yet, we know they have great potential. Garbarino in *Lost Boys* points out that part of the problem for young boys is not the breakdown of the family but the breakdown in the family. Family values. How does a young person learn how to direct his/her life through a sophisticated world of conflict and confusion? Media and technology influence fashion, art, music, and education. Parents, along with teachers, politicians, movie stars, music industry artists, and friends/peers all expose young people to different values models. All children need positive influences. They need to understand how to make decisions, form opinions and take action based on what *they* believe is right. Young people wonder what and how to think, believe, and behave. We live in a confusing culture, forced to make decisions about how to live our lives. Our children, our students experience confusion and conflict regarding politics, friends, money, school, love, sex, rules, authority, work, and material possessions. Additionally, we live in a complex culture, one that has now experienced terrorism here at home. Yet, we are invested as a country in keeping a global perspective, attempting to accept diversity and work toward achieving peace in the world and sustainability of our planet.

Sometimes teachers and other professionals offer a set of expectations and values that differ from those of students' families. We expect a student to transition into an independent setting and develop his/her own value system that may, in fact, emerge as a different set of values from those presented in the family. If educators expect students to truly learn for understanding and demonstrate that understanding, while a parent expects good grades or the students will lose his/her right to have an automobile, a values conflict arises.

We need to help our children, our students establish a sense of future: a future orientation. College learning disabled students have often told me they simply need to earn a degree. Bring home a degree. This is their parents' expectation. My expectation as their adviser is that they will journey through courses, learn, get excited about some area of study, seek out more knowledge and identify a career path that is a match to their abilities, interests, and lifelong learning interests. It is critical that students think not about the notion of "getting good grades" to please parents and insure their continuation in school, but about the relevance of their academic learning and experiences.

Particularly in higher education, there exists an attitude that students ought not be in college if they are not ready to accept the responsibilities of attending classes, doing their work on time, and studying. But we are living in a different world and culture. As faculty, it is too simplistic for us to carry that attitude into our classrooms. As teachers and educators, it must be our responsibility to offer our students not only opportunities for cognitive growth, but also experiences and thought provoking activities to help students develop a sense of purposefulness. Once students have a sense of this purposefulness, there is understanding; understanding of the gestalt, of how and why everything fits together: why we ask students to take specific courses, why we challenge them, why we expect them to inquire, why we push them to work hard, and why we have expectations for them and future generations.

Who is to teach them this? Whose responsibility is it to help them along this journey of self-discovery? Who will help them attempt to find meaning in every task? Who should ask them to question the values of their parents and decide if they, are in sync with family expectations? Who will help the student learn about what life truly means for him/her? And, who will help the student begin this journey of self-reflection and self-understanding? Current research has been published stating that 80% of our young people classified as juvenile delinquents do not have life plans. How do young people learn about important values within a society, and how does a young person become attached to and involved with a community culture, e.g., the culture and climate of a college campus, of a workplace, of an organization? How does a young person begin to think about and develop a life plan? Some students find this help through a college counselor or educational consultant. These professionals, during the later high school years, begin to question and guide the student though inventories to begin to determine a match for a post-secondary experience. A connection is established.

Once in a college, advising by university department personnel/faculty is critical. Advisors, once a student has declared a major, don't necessarily challenge the student to think about other academic or career options. The advising tends to consist of filling out a schedule for the following semester. Thus, prior to declaring a major, students should use their semester experiences to explore and talk with many people, other students, and student/residential life professionals who have an allegiance to a particular program or academic department. For learning disabled college freshmen, someone in the academic resource center or academic or career counseling department should be able to offer either testing, or informal diagnostic inquiry inventories to help the student begin to explore options based on that particular student's strengths and interests. This is a critical component of advising. Advising should not consist of a checklist for graduation. It is an opportunity for a student to connect with someone who might be a key figure for four years. This individual might offer support and guidance and truly be the connection the student needs and uses throughout the duration of his/her college experience. College academic advisor Pat Kowalchick who has worked with freshmen and students on academic probation in college views her role as advocate/teacher/support liaison. "The primary role of the academic advisor is to connect the student to the university. While suggesting courses and setting up schedules are functions of the advisor, in many universities, web-based programs will eventually provide these services as we soar into the 21st century. The connections the advisor makes with each student, and the connection to other university support services that the advisor assists the student in establishing, are the empowering tools that will enable each student to take ownership of his/her career."

Perhaps it is the director of a community service organization in high school who works with students to find an internship placement or a volunteer position. An appropriate connection during high school can create a possible link between student and teacher, or student and community member. Discussions concerning post-secondary options can emerge from these informal relationships or connections.

In *Succeeding Against the Odds: How the Leaning Disabled Can Realize Their Promise,* Sally Smith reminds us that, "Specialists in learning disabilities continue to hear from former students, even some from decades before. These students seem to need to keep in touch with those who knew them when." The connection was established and is maintained.

Now, with this said, there is another consideration. Let's entertain the possibility of an alternative route to college at 18 for the learning disabled student. What other post-secondary opportunities exist? Certainly one option for the high school graduate is to find a guidance counselor, college counselor, or educational consultant and through that professional consider identifying and locating potential work experiences in the home-based regional area while concurrently taking a course or two at a community college. Many community colleges offer support for learning-disabled students. For some students, this offers an appropriate alternative to full-time university work away from home and family support. It can be considered a transition semester or year. Community service or volunteer work or any other experiences that help students identify interest areas or potential career tracks and provide a year or more for general social and emotional development and maturation, are great alternatives to a college experience immediately following high school graduation.

Andi O'Hearn, IECA consultant shares this thought, "College is a major investment in a child's future. Taking a year off that is well structured, and offers opportunities to explore possible career options can help a student mature and enter college with a clear direction. With an end goal firmly in mind, a learning disabled student progresses more easily though required courses that without the year off program, may have seemed irrelevant. They have a better sense of where they are going and how they are going to get there."

How do learning disabled students identify their strengths, passions, and interests? A good educational evaluation is the first step. Asking reflective questions is another. What are my strengths? Weaknesses? Do I want to go to college? Why? Based on my interests would a vocational program be better suited for me? What kind of work do I enjoy doing? Do I like working with my hands? Do I like computers? Do I like working with people? Do I need to be outdoors? What kind of structure do I need in my life to succeed? What do others say about my strengths or talents? These questions provide a format for students to begin to self examine.

Vocational assessments should be available within high school settings. If a student has graduated from high school, state vocational rehabilitation agencies offer assessments. Educational consultants can also offer testing and inventories to help students explore their potential.

Transition programs exist for learning disabled students who need help making the transition from living at home to living independently. post-secondary day and residential transitional programs exist offering services from academic skill development to self-care and employment skill development. Internship volunteer positions and mentoring possibilities are other considerations. Teachers often befriend and mentor students. According to Dr. Mel Levine in *A Mind At A Time*, we should celebrate students' who "march to their own drummers" and "empower kids to arrive at. . . . self-affirming conclusions. We must celebrate their distinctiveness to say nothing of their valiant social courage." Mentors can help students identify their affinities and suggest strategies for students to develop those interests or passions. Mentors can be teachers, coaches, counselors, therapists, clergy, neighbors, or, like Dr. Mel Levine, physicians. Students who struggle with social behavior or social independence can learn by shadowing an adult who models appropriate social interchanges. These opportunities can be in, or outside the classroom, in work or internship experiences. "It can be hard to go it alone when you're feeling inadequate. Many struggling students can benefit from an interaction with a professional who can offer them ongoing advice and advocacy." (Levine 289)

It is important to remember that many steps are necessary to the growth that takes place after high school. Dr. Corinne Smith and Lisa Strick in their book, *Learning Disabilities A-Z: A Parent's Complete Guide to Learning Disabilities from Preschool to Adulthood* remind us that we need to stay connected to, support, and motivate our young people though the post-secondary experiences. "Research finds that substantial numbers of individuals with learning disabilities do not achieve economic independence until they are in their middle to late twenties, and that the education and employment histories are often characterized by many wrong turns and false starts. While watching youngsters flounder can be frustrating and sometimes frightening, parents must remember that many of these young people learn best by trial and error; they simply don't know what they like or can do until they try it." Once again the challenge is to support, connect, and lead our children toward the realistic and possible options that exist for them.

Whatever choices our children make after high school, we (educators and parents) should all consider:

- Where and how our children might find "meaningfulness" in their lives: Will it be through a work experience, through a vocational internship, within a computer technology course, in a community college setting or back-packing through the United States?
- Post-secondary placements or experiences must focus on learning and meaning, not on information learned in isolation. Learning should be interdisciplinary or holistic.
- Where or how will the students learn to put failure or failures in their correct perspective?
- How will students continue to expand their growth in the area of moral development?
- What experiences can continue to offer opportunities to help our young people develop a sense of responsibility?
- How will we encourage our children to make good decisions and use appropriate judgment?
- What skills can we teach our children to help them make programmatic transitions with less stress?

We must remember that our young people are different from those of prior generations. They are the products of a culture grounded in excessive television, immediate technology, dietary changes, violence and transient neighborhoods, in a time of terrorism with the threat of war. Yet, they are full of hope. They are optimistic and believe they can be successful. In a January 1998 speech, researcher and author Jeanette S. Cureton described a new generation "that is desperately clinging to its dreams, but their hope, though broadly professed is fragile. Their lives are being challenged at every turn: in their families, their communities, their nation, and their world. What is remarkable is that their hopes have not been engulfed by their fears."

Many Shades for Success

Chapter Six

To Serve or Not to Serve

Kathryn D. Zachary, M.Ed.

Volunteer Specialist and Vesodot Program Assistant

That is the question, isn't it? Can children who have disabilities find meaningful volunteer or service learning positions and give back to their communities? Should they look for volunteer work, or is their time better spent looking for paid employment? What if it's just not practical for young adults with disabilities to seek employment? How do young adults with disabilities gain experience, prepare resumes and obtain paid employment?

Many barriers prevent young adults with disabilities from gaining access to employment, including lack of life experiences. One of the largest barriers is that young adults with disabilities may not be aware of the opportunities that exist right in their own communities. Other barriers include misconceptions on the parts of the organizations looking for volunteers. Often these organizations fear the cost of accommodations would be prohibitive. This simply is not the case. Most accommodations can be provided for free or for low cost, generally under $50.00. Also, volunteers with disabilities frequently have their own access equipment. Other perceived barriers are that young adults with disabilities will require more supervision and need more training. According to the study on Barriers to the Inclusion of Volunteers with Developmental Disabilities by Miller, Schleien, & Bedini, 2003; 66% of those surveyed in this study indicated that a lack of staff or that staff with minimal training was a barrier. Transportation has also proven a barrier for young adults with disabilities. One program called Living, Learning and Leading found this to be a particularly difficult issue. This program was designed to work with young adults with disabilities, ages 14–22, to find them volunteer opportunities within their communities. Once those opportunities were found, the participants in the program were connected with career-support mentors. Of those who volunteered to be mentors, many were disabled themselves who relied on public transportation, limiting the geographical range where they could serve, as well as their reliability and availability to serve. Supporting this observation are the results of a study done by Miller, Schleien & Bedini in 2003 that found 56% of those surveyed indicated transportation was a barrier.

It is possible to find a meaningful volunteer or service learning position for the young adult with disabilities, whether the disabilities are emotional, physical, or cognitive. The key is to be selective and to research the options. Initially, the young adults must decide whether they want a service learning experience or a volunteer position. A straight volunteer experience is one where no formal processing or debriefing of the work is done. One example would be young adults volunteering at a food pantry. They would go about their assigned duties and leave when it was appropriate for them to do so. Service learning can be defined as a volunteer experience guided by someone, with the participants given time to process and debrief the experience through discussion and/or journal writing. Many school systems participate in this kind of volunteer work. Frequently in the upper grades, some kind of volunteer service is required for graduation. Both kinds of volunteer experience can be rewarding and beneficial.

Basic human needs include a sense of belonging, accomplishment, and a reliable social network. Most of all, young adults need to develop a sense of self worth. they must prove their worth to themselves, their families, and their communities by contributing in some fashion. Often young adults with disabilities are isolated; their friends may be other youths with disabilities, and they may reside in group-homes with limited activities. Volunteering as a group from the residence doesn't allow for the personal development of friends outside that closed community. Volunteering is one way of addressing these issues.

Volunteering can provide a less stressful introduction to the world of work, as it is largely non-competitive. Volunteer positions can also be flexible when it comes to the number of hours that are required. Many volunteer jobs can be tailored to meet the needs of the volunteer's transportation requirements, medical appointments, or after school activities. The consequences of absenteeism are considerably reduced at a volunteer job. A volunteer position may be longer lasting and more secure, especially in a tight labor market, and there are always openings available in a wide variety of situations.

Many studies have been done that support the following information (Morgan & Strebb, (undated); Westheimer & Kahne, 2000; Anderson, 1998; Kirby, 2001; Muscott, et al. 1999; Rosenberg, McKeon & Dinero, 1999. Some of the other benefits are outlined below.

Before Volunteering	While Volunteering and After
Behavior—Acting out, isolating, poor school work performance	Makes effort to control behavior, less isolating, improved school work performance
Poor self-esteem	Increased self-esteem
Lack of self-confidence	Improved self-confidence
Little or no work history, no work skills	Gains experience for resume, acquires skills

Feelings of helplessness	Gains satisfaction in learning to help others
Isolation from the community	Becomes an active member of the community and develops friendships
Lack of a job focus	Learns likes and dislikes in world of work
No leadership skills	Develops leadership skills
Has little team work skills	Gets experience working as part of a team, learns to appreciate working as part of a team
Little access to role models	Benefits from exposure to more and different role models

When young adults are looking for volunteer work of any kind, they need to keep several things in mind. The first consideration is to investigate positions that will hold their interest. If they like sports, then the experience should be based around sports. One of the mantras in the volunteer world is that volunteers have to like what they are doing to be successful and to maintain their interest. As the young adults get older or closer to graduation from high school, their volunteer experiences can be molded so they contain vocational components. For instance, if the goal is to increase office skills such as filing, shredding, photocopying, phone answering, or data entry, organizations requiring office support need to be sought out so volunteers can learn those skills.

Non-profits are the biggest source of volunteer jobs. Because their resources are limited, they use volunteers for a variety of job opportunities. There are many ways to locate a potential volunteer position. One way is to search on the World Wide Web simply using "volunteer" as a search term. Several websites act as clearinghouses for volunteer positions.

- www.idealist.org
- www.volunteermatch.org
- www.opportunitynocs.org
- www.unitedway.org
- www.craigslist.org
- www.volunteersolutions.org

These are just a few of the sites that are available. This is not an exhaustive list, nor are these recommended above others that may be found. Another way to search on the web is to locate the web pages of non-profits in the volunteer's area. Often these sites list volunteer positions. One hint is to check under employment opportunities if there is no option for volunteer work. One more method is to look in the phone book under associations, since many charities and civic groups are listed that way. Sometimes in the front of the phone book, social service organizations are listed that serve the local community; these are also potential sources. Looking in newspapers, particularly local ones, is another option. Volunteer positions are sometimes listed in the classified section. If the disability is represented by a national association, such as the Cerebral Palsy Association, the organization tends to use volunteers with that disability and it knows how to compensate for the disability. Therefore, these organizations are rich resources for young adults with disabilities seeking volunteer opportunities.

In addition, word of mouth is an excellent resource for locating volunteer jobs. Other parents, parent-support, and local school groups provide a good beginning. Also, local or state agencies help individuals obtain volunteer placements. One such program, Youth Ability in Boston and nine other cities across the United States, serves young adults with disabilities, ages 14–22, finding them volunteer opportunities within their communities. Living, Learning and Leading is another program in Boston with similar goals. This program also works with young adults with disabilities. Once the volunteer position is secured, the participant is connected with a career support mentor.

When a volunteer job of interest has been found, the next step is to do some research on that organization and ask many questions to find out is if their services are accessible for the volunteer's particular needs. If not, are they willing and able to work out the issues of accommodation? The following questions can be asked to decide if the volunteer position is the right match and have been adapted from *Making a Good Match: Questions for Volunteers and Organizations to Ask,* by Jill Murray in Impact v14 (2) p9.

Questions for volunteers to ask themselves:	Questions for volunteers to ask organizations:
• Will I be able to make a meaningful contribution through this? Do I want to volunteer for something I am already interested in? Do I want to learn something new? • Do I believe my work has value? • Will it be recognized? • Why do I want to volunteer my time instead of getting paid?	• Will you tell me what to expect in this volunteer position? • Is this real work with responsibilities and accountability? • Does your staff believe I am a valuable member of the team? • What experience does your staff have working with people with disabilities?

• Do I have time to offer? What is the time commitment? What is the length of service?	• If I have any problems with duties, my supervisor, or support issues, who is my contact?
• Do I support the organization's goals?	• Who would listen to me if I had ideas or shared perspectives on how the organization could improve?
• What will I learn through this volunteer experience?	• Will you give me the supports I need to do the job you expect?
• Do I want to volunteer with a disability-related agency?	• Have others with disabilities volunteered here before?
• Do I want to work where I can educate others about issues of people with disabilities?	• Can I call a past volunteer to get a reference?
• Do I want to find a place that will link me to a new area or group?	• If this position is not the best match for me, how should I tell you?
• Does the organization ever hire anyone with disabilities?	• If you think I could do a better job, how will you tell me?

Once the decision to volunteer at a particular organization has been made, the next step is to look at the volunteer job being offered and decide if it is a good match in location, interest, and personality. If the volunteer position is not doable, one option to consider is a job carve. Job carving is taking the position in question and breaking it down into its component parts. Once the component parts have been identified, the next step is to decide what parts can be done by the young adult and what other parts of the position can be done by another volunteer or employee. For example, if the organization is looking for receptionist support that includes telephone work, photocopying, and mail delivery, but the potential volunteer is non-verbal, a solution is to have the volunteer do the mail delivery and/or the photocopying.

The following should be considered before agreeing to take the volunteer job:

- Can the volunteer job be done as it stands? If not, can a job carve be done?
- Are accommodations required?
- Does the volunteer already have the necessary materials for the accommodation, or will the organization be asked to supply them?

For the first time in their lives, volunteers with disabilities are being helpful and needed rather then the recipients of services. This is poignantly demonstrated by Rachel's story.

Rachel's story:

Rachel is a homeless 22 year-old who has a brain injury sustained in a car accident at age 19. It left her with seizures, short-term memory loss, sensitivity to stimuli, difficulty with balance, and vertigo. Adding to an already frustrating situation, her disability is invisible. Rachel, who is neat, clean and articulate, receives social services; but because of the long wait for housing, she has not been able to find a place to live. She receives medical care for her brain injury and is currently undergoing rehabilitation for the injury. Prior to the accident, she had a job as a pharmacy tech' for four years. After the accident she attempted to go back to work, resulting in nine jobs over a 16-month period.

She stays connected to the world via the Internet at public libraries, and college and university libraries. According to Rachel, "I walk right in. I have a backpack on; so they think I belong there." While on the Internet, Rachel came across the Living, Learning and Leading program and decided to give it a chance.

Rachel believes that volunteering has been helpful to her. She states, "It gives me something to do, helps with my self-esteem, and gives me experience to put on a resume. It's better than doing nothing, and it forces me to make my brain work. Volunteering allows me to work on skills that I have lost, such as memory and attention span." Currently Rachel works with children who are seriously ill.

Rachel is serious about her recovery, which is evident when she states; "I need something to challenge me because of the brain injury. Working in stimulating environments is hard, and I easily become over-stimulated; but I have to push myself, or I will never be able to hold a regular job."

One aspect of volunteering that Rachel feels has helped is having the Career Support Mentor. She believes that it is helpful to be able to talk with someone who expects her to do something and has more work experience than she does.

Rachel is confident that volunteering will eventually lead to employment, but for right now feels that it is the best thing for her to do for several other reasons. She states, "It lets me work on skills I have lost without the pressure of real employment. It's easier to volunteer during my recovery because I can be absent, and they won't fire me like they would at a regular job. They are more willing to work with you because you are doing them a service."

When asked how she thought the program (volunteering) in general was helpful to young adults, she replied, "It's good for kids because

* Names have been changed to protect privacy.

you're stuck with who your friends are, and they are either the ones in your class or the ones you live with." Rachel also feels it is helpful because "not many people are willing to hire people with disabilities. This way they get to try them out and get over their stereotypical thinking." Rachel continues her volunteer work to gain more experience for her resume and to learn how to compensate for some of the skills she has lost.

Rachael's story demonstrates issues parents, educators and service providers worry about when it comes to paid employment.

Bob's story:

Bob is a 20-something young man with learning disabilities. When Bob decided to volunteer, he was unemployed. He had previously worked in communications and marketing, but was unsure if he could have gotten the volunteer position on his own. Bob stated that the program "gave me a place to go and a sense of structure. You can only send out so many resumes, and then you have to do something else. If I hadn't been volunteering, I would be home watching television."

Bob volunteered working with adults who were English speakers of other languages (ESOL), learning to speak English. He also helped people with disabilities. Bob feels that by volunteering he got to explore different vocational areas, which increased his self-esteem because he found out that there were many things that he could do. Bob stated that with volunteering there is more flexibility and you can focus more on what your interests are. He also feels that if you didn't like what you were doing as a volunteer you could change but that in a paid position, this would be more difficult. Bob relates a story where the teacher of the ESOL class asked him to co-teach a class. He says that he was very nervous but the class was eager to learn and that made it okay. This experience increased his self-confidence and gave him teaching experience. Bob reports that he increased his skill level in many areas including interpersonal, communication, public speaking and patience.

Bob says, "Volunteering helped me decide to go back to school and opened up my eyes to what my target audience will be, and now I know I want to focus on kids." Bob went on to say, "If I hadn't volunteered I would probably be in a job I hated."

Now majoring in social services and planning to work with children with emotional, behavioral, and learning disabilities in a residential setting, Bob feels that his volunteering and the experience of his own disability have led him to provide the support to others that will empower them to be successful. Bob thinks "sometimes people with disabilities are looked down upon as severely disabled. But people with disabilities can do jobs, just differently and sometimes better than normal people, because they are more willing to learn, and success is so much more gratifying."

Both young adults have pointed out the need for more volunteer opportunities for those with disabilities. Their experience demonstrates the benefits of volunteering, such as being able to try out new vocations, flexibility of scheduling, and having structure. Rachel's and Bob's stories show the emotional growth volunteering provides. Their experiences support the idea that volunteering can be a powerful tool in the development of the young adult with disabilities.

Many Shades for Success

Chapter Seven

Planning Ahead Helping Your Teen Transition From School to Work

Ruth M. Antonucci, M.A., C.A.G.S.

Director of Job Training and Employment, Easter Seals Massachusetts

School-to-work transition planning is an essential component of any student's high school life, and students with disabilities should plan early to ensure their goals can be met. Social attitudes are changing toward people with disabilities, recognizing both the possibility and importance of successful employment for them. As attitudes change and opportunities broaden for employment of people with disabilities, parents will play an increasingly significant role in preparing students with disabilities for post-secondary training and employment. Everyone, especially young adults, can appreciate how a job leads to independence, a stronger sense of self-esteem, and accomplishment. Their goal should be a satisfying job; one that fits their skills and interests and offers employment opportunity. A parent's role is to help their children plan early, support their dreams, and help guide the process of transition. By being aware of the choices and issues the student will face, families will have more time to plan, explore, and learn what options are available.

This guide discusses two major steps that help in the early planning of the transition process:

Vocational Assessments: a process designed to help students and parents understand the student's job-related skills, interests and preferences. This helps set direction for all future planning.

Job Supports: include the skills necessary to identify a career path and find a job, as well as the soft-skills required to keep a job.

The school will generally incorporate these services into an IEP – and parents and students can help by providing as much information as possible about the student's desires. Vocational assessments and job supports are described below the transition planning chart.

Use the following chart as a general guideline for transition planning:

Student's Age	Students' Activity	Parents' Activity
12 and under	• Watch parents and friends at work • Dream of what you want to do	• Let children help out around the house • Discuss different jobs
12-14	• Think about what you like to do and what you are good at • Tell your parents and teachers what classes you like the best • Share your hobbies with others	• Encourage children to talk about school subjects and ask how these can relate to jobs • Support all ideas for potential jobs

14	• Attend all IEP meetings—you are an important member of the team • Learn about the responsibilities of different jobs • Know you can work in a job you will love • Ask questions if you don't understand something • Start taking control of your future by speaking up—be your own advocate	• Start asking children what they see as a vocational goal • Keep the child's vision and dream alive—realistic goals can grow from dreams • Know your child should participate in the IEP meetings—and support him • Know the options for vocational planning and assessments • Focus IEP meetings on the future—including course schedules to • support career goals
16+	• Your goals, dreams and job choices should be known by the team • Ask about job opportunities—internships too • Talk with your team and family about how your disability may impact the job you want—and learn about the different types of accommodations available • A two-year transition plan should be made two years before you graduate—so be comfortable with all services • A vocation assessment will help you identify your strengths, interests, and job preferences • Consider [job shadowing" to learn about a job—you will follow and observe someone doing the job you are interested in	• By 16, the statement of required transitional services should be included in the IEP—this includes vocational assessments and job supports • Make sure your child's interests, preferences and skills are being addressed • At 18, your child is fully responsible for making decisions about education services and transition plans • Continue to support and encourage your child to volunteer to gain valuable work experience, and work after school and summers
Graduation	• Find your job! Ask for assistance from parents, agencies and others—networking helps make the job search easier	• Your school will have provided a transition plan into adult services for your student—take advantage of all assistance

Within the past 20 years, there has been consistent evidence that youth with disabilities are more likely to drop out of high school, less likely to pursue post-secondary education, and less likely to be employed than are youth without disabilities. In fact, 22% of youth with disabilities fail to complete high school, compared to 9% of those without disabilities (National Organization on Disabilities, 2002).

Teenagers with disabilities do not have the same opportunities as their able-bodied peers for getting that all-important first after-school or summer job. There are many barriers – both attitudinal and physical. However, the early work experience develops the skills and attitudes that lead to future success in the workplace. Lack of this experience among teens with disabilities is a major factor in their high unemployment rate as adults.

While school-to-work transition planning has started to emerge as a recognized service for students with special needs, implementation for younger children with disabilities is innovative, necessary, and a realistic aspect of life planning for these individuals. Parents must be their children's best advocates in the area of transition planning. Even though the Individuals with Disabilities Act (IDEA) guarantees by law services for students ages 3 to 21, or until they graduate high school whichever comes first, an effective learning environment and transition planning do not happen by chance. These laws are only meaningful when parents know about them and can use the proper processes to assure that such services are provided in a timely manner for their child.

Early transition planning helps both parents and students educate themselves so they can actively contribute to the student's success by ensuring the student has every opportunity to reach his/her highest potential. The ultimate purpose is to help students with disabilities become active, contributing members of their communities.

In this process, the parents must assume the roles of both advocates and collaborators. Parents must make sure that transition planning is an ongoing part of their child's career development plans. Most importantly, the student should be involved in transitional planning. Making the student part of the planning team can be vital in motivating the student in school and in developing his or her self-advocacy skills and independence. School-to-work transition planning should ensure that the curriculum of each student includes learning about career options.

Vocational success is a realistic, achievable goal for children with disabilities. Education for schools and parents can only enhance that goal. The first step is to identify the student's interests and skills. This entails use of the vocational assessment.

Vocational Assessment: Purposes and Benefits

One tool that can be of considerable help is the vocational assessment. Vocational assessment can provide the information needed to match the student's abilities and interests to appropriate career goals and training programs. It also can identify the services required by the student to make the transition from school to work as smooth and successful as possible.

The purpose of vocational evaluations is to assist individual students with the career planning process. The process includes collecting information about the student's educational background, interests, preferences, hobbies, skills, aptitudes, and personal goals. This information is gathered through various methods, including one-to-one interviewing and self-assessment techniques, as well as standardized interest testing. Standardized tests may include *the Strong Campbell Interest Inventory, the Nelson-Denny Reading Comprehension Test, the Wide Range Achievement Test, the Minnesota Manual Dexterity Test, and the Lafayette Grooved Pegboard.*

A complete vocational assessment process typically consists of three to four hour sessions over a period of up to three days. Results of the vocational assessment are then presented to the student's team, comprised of the evaluator, the student, the teacher, and any other individuals the student or school choose to invite. Results of the assessment are reviewed and recommendations are made regarding an appropriate vocational goal and activities to achieve that goal. Final recommendations for future planning involve input from all team members at that session. Input from the student, relevant family members, and other people important to the student is critical when considering all aspects of the individual's life. A comprehensive vocational assessment report is typically generated within two weeks of the evaluation. The report discusses detailed results of the interview, testing results, and recommendations.

Vocational assessment provides information on the student's
- Career development background
- Interests
- Aptitudes
- Special needs
- Learning style
- Work habits and behaviors
- Personal and social skills
- Values and attitudes toward work
- Self-concept
- Work tolerances

Through the assessment process, parents and professionals learn about the student, and the student learns about himself or herself. Students generally emerge from the vocational assessment process with increased self-awareness and a better understanding of their skills. When students are being assessed they often may:[1]

- Want to discuss their vocational or career futures or specific vocational education plans
- Show excitement about the vocational activities on which they are working
- Enthusiastically talk with their families and friends about what they are doing
- in school
- Develop new, realistic career interests
- Exhibit more self-confidence and self-esteem
- Show more interest in school and in their academic performance

The active participation of students in the assessment process is an important factor in demonstrating how school relates to future work opportunities. This also helps to motivate them during the school years. Learning about various jobs, trying out work roles, exploring interests, and getting feedback on many different aspects of individual abilities and performance broaden students' knowledge base of the work-world and themselves. This allows them to explore which careers might be appropriate for them and to identify those that are not. Furthermore, the school can support the student's interest through curriculum choices.

Even for students with disabilities who plan to attend college, vocational assessment is an important process in identifying post-secondary and career options. It is a useful first step for students with disabilities planning to participate in vocational education programs. Often, a student is preparing for a school-to-work transition but discovers a career path requiring further schooling. In these cases, vocational assessment actually raises the bar for their personal expectations and allows the student to progress even farther then he or she realized was possible.

The vocational assessment will assist and empower the student (and his or her advocates) in making decisions regarding work and the training or services needed to gain employment. The benefits of gathering—and using—this information are many. Among these are career awareness and exploration, improved self-awareness and motivation, development of a vocational profile, and identification of realistic short- and

1. *Vocational Assessment: A Guide For Parents and Professionals.* National Information Center for Children and Youth with Disabilities (NICHCY) Transition Summary #TS6, December, 1990

long-term career goals. These goals are more realistic because they are based upon who the student is as an individual and what he or she is capable of and interested in doing.

As a student prepares to graduate, parents should be aware that vocational assessment will continue to be important for a young adult's successful transition to independence in either employment or post-secondary training. In addition to identifying specific transition needs, career plans, and goals, vocational assessment can assist parents and professionals in making referrals for adult services. For many young adults with disabilities, state-sponsored vocational rehabilitation services or other community-based services may be realistic options. The information gathered through the assessment process can help the individual with a disability, his or her family, and the employer identify the accommodations or assistance needed for getting and keeping a job.

PARENTS AND THE VOCATIONAL ASSESSMENT PROCESS

Parents have critical roles to play in the vocational planning process. Here, as in all aspects of the student's education, parents are the prime advocates and advisors. There are both general and specific tasks parents can perform to help before and throughout the vocational assessment process.

First, parents should recognize that vocational assessments may or may not be taking place in the school system and can range from informal to quite comprehensive. Parents should be prepared to ask school personnel about what vocational assessment services are available and whether they are provided within the school system itself or through an outside agency, such as a local rehabilitation facility or the state division of vocational rehabilitation.

If the school does have services available, parents should identify how students can be referred for participation. This is best done early in a child's education—at age 14. If services are provided through an outside agency, parents should request that the school guidance counselor, special education, or transition teacher investigate where and how these services can be accessed. Here are some additional suggestions for parents:[2]

- Acquaint your son or daughter with as many occupations as possible, by visiting job sites, accompanying family, and friends to work, and exploring how jobs contribute to the community
- Assign chores that encourage the development of responsibility and mastery of independent living skills
- Encourage your son or daughter to take pre-vocational courses

2. *Transition Planning" A Team Effort.* National Information Center for Children and Youth with Disabilities (NICHCY) Transition Summary 10 (TS10) 1999, Resources Updated, 2002

- Request that your son's or daughter's school program include career education, such as class presentations about various careers, career fairs, or career research activities
- Request that class work include career exploration and preparation activities, such as job shadowing, in-school work experience and community job internships
- Arrange for summer work experience for your son or daughter, either volunteer or paid employment

In this process, parents must assume the roles of both advocates and collaborators. Parents must make sure that transition planning is an ongoing part of their child's career development plans. Most importantly, the student should be involved in transitional planning. Making the student part of the planning team can be vital in motivating the student in school and in developing his or her self-advocacy skills and independence. School-to-work transition planning should ensure that the curriculum of each student includes learning about career options.

Job Supports: tools to support a vocational goal

Once a career goal is established based on interests, preferences and realistic goals, students and parents can embark on the next journey—finding the right job. Job supports can include anything that provides assistance in searching for jobs, identifying the perfect job, job etiquette, and understanding the specifics of career path opportunity. Schools may partner with other agencies as well as a student's family to provide the following services.

Job-Seeking Skills

A job placement specialist (teacher/parent, etc.) works with the student to prepare him or her for the competitive work force. Topics discussed are appropriate work behavior, including office etiquette, office attire, and co-worker relations. The topics can also include a discussion of the interview process and techniques. Students are walked through resume and cover letter preparation, in addition to exploring where to look for a job. The specialist prepares the student for the one-on-one job placement component and makes sure that any identified obstacles to employment have been addressed and resolved. At the same time, the student's IEP team should be meeting. The team has worked closely with the student and should be aware of particular work behaviors that will need to be addressed in the workshops. The team may suggest incentives for students to be successful in this phase.

Job Shadowing

1. The student sits with a job placement specialist and reviews goals

and vocational evaluation findings. Together, they should outline up to five employers to visit within the student's geographic region. The visits allow the student to observe others performing job duties similar to his or her vocational goals. The student is encouraged to ask questions of these business people and workers.

2. As a follow-up to these visits, the placement specialist and student discuss their observations, questions, concerns, and general thoughts. Training for these types of positions, job duties, career outlook, and general trends in the region are explored. The goal of this discussion is to identify two sites that were a good match to the student's interests, skills, and abilities.

3. The placement specialist and the student should arrange second visits to the two locations. These visits are more job-specific, in that the student will be able to shadow someone in the company who has a job that he or she is interested in pursuing. The opportunity to ask more specific questions and possibly have a hands-on experience is explored. Approximately one to two hours are spent on-site for these second visits.

4. Following the second visits, the student should be able to make an informed career choice and develop a path for attaining competitive employment.

Job Placement

Ultimately, the students work with the job placement specialist to obtain a job they want that matches their abilities and preferences. The placement specialist, student, and employer then determine if individualized job coaching will be necessary.

Job Coaching

The goal is for the student to function independently within the work environment. The first step to achieving that goal is the designation of an external job coach, as defined by the team. The second step is to explore natural supports: other employees who work with the student and will provide assistance and guidance when needed.

ANN'S DREAM

How do you help a 14 1/2 year-old 8th grader with cerebral palsy and visual deficits achieve her dream job? Ann's school was presented with this challenge when this determined student was referred for a vocational evaluation. Her school, taking a progressive approach, facilitated the collaboration among their team, outside agencies and the student. The objective was clear: to help Ann identify a personal vocational goal and develop the best plan possible to attain the goal. The school then could productively use the high school years to provide the best curriculum for Ann's chosen career path.

A vocational evaluation was performed to assess Ann's interests, preferences, aptitudes and learning abilities. The following accommodations were made to promote Ann's independence in participating in the assessment:

- enlarged printed test material
- laptop
- Testing material either scanned or created for computer use
- Document holder with line minder

The assessment ultimately supported the student's desire to work in a care-giving field. The following recommendations were made:

1. Student to focus on academics
2. Student to explore volunteering opportunities at a local hospital
3. Student to complete an assistive technology evaluation to assess
   - computer usage
   - mounting system needs
   - software and hardware needs

This collaboration helped prepare this student for a valuable, fruitful, and enriching career. Ann was able to achieve her goals by being provided the personalized tools to boost self-esteem, focus on attainable career paths, and fully develop an independent mindset of happiness and success.

GREG'S SUCCESS

As a senior in high school, this 18-year-old student with spina bifida was ready to stretch his wings and start looking for a career that fulfilled his ultimate desire to work with animals. He was referred for a vocational evaluation with the specific appeal of helping him to determine a realistic vocational goal.

Greg expressed an interest in becoming a veterinarian. The core of his vocational assessment included situational assessments, along with standardized interest and academic testing. The situational assessment process provided an opportunity for Greg to explore his abilities and aptitudes in a hands-on manner.

The evaluation did not support Greg's goal of being a veterinarian. However, opportunities were identified for him to experience other career options in industries that specifically cater to animals to create that link in his career goal. Job shadowing services were recommended to reinforce his desires. The purpose of job shadowing is to provide a student with an opportunity to observe and ask questions about various jobs within a career field. In Greg's case, he visited:

- a pet supply store

- veterinarian's office
- service dog organization

Greg had an opportunity to observe, ask questions and try hands-on tasks so that he was able to make an informed choice regarding his career goal. Greg opted for work in the pet supply store. He continues to increase his hours there and is training to increase his job responsibilities within the retail setting. Greg has his learner's permit and is saving money to adapt the family van with hand controls so he can drive to work.

WHAT'S NEXT?

Planning for Employment—What Do These Students Need? [3]

- *Assessment*, which identifies current strengths, needs, interests, and preferences for post-school employment, independent living, and post-secondary training and education
- *Development* of job and job placement options and awareness of skills needed
- *Matching* of the student with a job
- School- and work-based *training and preparation*
- *Placement and follow-up*

ACTIONS FOR A SMOOTH SCHOOL-TO-WORK TRANSITION

For assessment:

- Interview the student about vocational interests and preferences (use other methods to assess the interests and preferences of non-verbal students)
- Conduct a situational assessment (observation in a work setting) to assess endurance, strength, aptitude, social skills, interests, and interactions
- Perform a formal vocational evaluation conducted by a trained evaluator
- Encourage self-assessment by the student
- Develop the student's awareness of different jobs
- Discuss health care issues that may affect employment

For development:

- Analyze the local labor market (contact state employment services and request information for the region; contact the local vocational advisory council and chamber of commerce; review local want ads; contact employment agencies) to identify job openings and local labor needs

3. *Informal Assessments for Transition Planning.* Gary M. Clark James R. Patton Moulton, L. R. Publisher:200 by PRO-ED, Inc.

- Get a range of work experiences: explorations, job shadowing, mentoring, and internships
- Identify community programs offering job placement or training
- Build a network of employer and community program contacts
- Provide training to employers on issues related to employees with disabilities

For matching:
- Analyze the demands and expectations of the job site, such as the duties, skill requirements, hours, location, transportation, wages, benefits, and social skills
- List the supports the student needs to be successful on the job
- Match the student's assessment and the list of needed supports to the job demands, including transportation to the job
- Identify current gaps and needs for success
- Identify the necessary natural supports, job accommodations, adaptive equipment, and support services

For training and preparation:
- Teach the student job-seeking skills
- Provide community-based work experiences related to career development
- Identify potential service providers
- Provide natural supports and accommodations
- Provide instruction and training (pre-employment or on-the-job)

For placement and follow-up:
- Work with the employer to determine the employee's response to the job demands and identify strategies to capitalize on strengths and minimize limitations
- Provide natural supports and accommodations
- Monitor progress and readiness for job advancement
- Monitor the changing need for natural supports and make adjustments, as needed

CONCLUSION: TAKING CONTROL

To improve transition results for young people with disabilities, individual transition team members and community transition team members must work creatively. Here are some starting steps.

Students:
- Write down your long-term goals and what you think you need to do to reach them.

- Read your IEP and transition plan and determine if the plan is being implemented.
- Tell your teachers you want to lead your own IEP meeting and ask them to help you learn what to do.
- Learn about your civil rights under the law, such as the Americans with Disabilities Act.
- Learn about your disability, how to explain your strengths to people and how to ask for reasonable accommodations.
- Practice job interviews and asking for accommodations.
- Talk with your doctor and parents about your health care needs so you will be ready to take responsibility for them.
- Ask your teacher how to get involved with your community's transition team.

Family Members:
- Observe your son's or daughter's independent living skills, work behaviors, social involvement, dreams and hopes.
- Instill the concept of work, the impact work has on independence and the value of good work habits.
- Call your child's teachers and ask that transition services, including financial planning, be addressed at your next meeting.
- Help your child learn about his or her disability and how to ask for the supports he or she needs.
- Give your child responsibility for chores at home.
- Provide a weekly allowance, that will help create a link between money and independence.
- Role play different situations with your child, such as job interviews.
- Discuss your child's medical needs with him or her and facilitate discussions with your doctor.
- Introduce your child to adult role models with disabilities.

School or Agency Administrators:
- Evaluate transition services in your system.
- Look into establishing or strengthening your community transition team.
- Make a telephone call to develop a new community agency contact.
- Develop a cooperative agreement with another agency specifying how to coordinate transition.
- Encourage your staff to be creative in problem solving.

Special Educators:
- Talk to students and families about transition services.
- Ask to attend a conference, workshop, or other learning opportunity related to transition.
- Teach students about their civil rights under the law, such as the Americans with Disabilities Act.
- Pledge to conduct collaborative, needs-based IEP meetings that empower youth and families.
- Provide youth with systematic activities that familiarize them with the IEP process and prepare them to take active roles.

Thoughts and advice from a recent graduate:

Matthew, 23, has been working for over three years and is progressing regularly in job responsibilities. He recently started taking classes at a community college—his goal is to get his certificate in web design. He did not think he would be working full time in a job he loved, or taking college classes while he was in high school. His high school brought him to a sheltered workshop doing piece work assembly. That was when *he* decided to take control. He left the workshop, and took a computer class —following his hobby of computer games. He also job-shadowed in a few technical industries. His first job was in customer service/retail, which he kept for two years. His current job involves customer service in the financial sector. When Matthew was asked what advice he would give to parents and students in high school, he offered the following.

"Students should take the first step, even if it's a small one, to see what is out there that interests them. When students are younger, parents should support and ask what they want to do, but as the students gets near graduation, they have to take control."

Matthew goes on to say he "encourages high school students today to do something that interests them, spend time learning computers or something that is a hobby."

You can help your students attain a job that provides them independence and satisfaction. It is worth it!

RESOURCES & WEBSITES

Vocational Assessment: A Guide For Parents and Professionals
National Information Center for Children and Youth with Disabilities (NICHCY)
   Transition Summary #TS6, December, 1990
Transition Planning: A Team Effort
National Information Center for Children and Youth with Disabilities (NICHCY)
   Transition Summary 10 (TS10) 1999, Resources Updated, 2002
Informal Assessments for Transition Planning
Gary M. Clark James R. Patton Moulton, L. R Publisher: 200 by PRO-ED, Inc
www.transitionlink.com
www.transitioncoalition.org

Chapter Eight

Community Partnerships:
The Key to Independence

Betsey Parlato, M.A.

Executive Director, Chapel Haven, Inc. New Haven, CT

The Davis' anxiously awaited the birth of their first son. Their excitement could only be matched by the optimistic anticipation of what their lives would be like now as a family, rather than as a couple. However, soon after Ben's birth, the couple detected developmental delays. Visiting a variety of neurologists, they continued to hear the same dire predictions. All the specialists believed that Ben would never be able to learn. Today, however, 22 years later, Ben is learning and living independently hundreds of miles from his family's home.

The Davis' have devoted much of their life to creating relationships, within their community and beyond, that would foster Ben's growth toward independence. They recognized early that Ben would need the support of many people to be successful in life. Forging relationships became a family endeavor and enriched not only Ben's life, but also the lives of everyone involved with him.

Yet for some families of children with disabilities, life can become full of frustration and bitterness. Recognition of the disability, as with Ben, can occur early, sometimes as early as birth, and with it comes the fight for inclusion. For others, preschool or elementary school provides the first setting for a cognitive disability to be diagnosed. The child's entry into the classroom becomes an introduction to the challenges to come.

THE FIRST COMMUNITY PARTNERSHIP: THE SCHOOL

It is a great irony that just as the first opportunity a child has to experience a partnership is with the school, the first time a child is excluded from a community is also in the school. Schools and classrooms, unfortunately, provide the means by which students with disabilities can be cut off from "normal" children and excluded from the community. Whether it is classroom segregation or, exclusion based on academic performance, the special student is, from the start, reinforced neither by, the academic setting nor the community setting of his peers.

The elementary school years besiege the child and family with challenges and decisions at every turn. The child needs "accommodation," but the accommodation may take him out of the community, emotionally if not physically. If the family is reluctant to acknowledge the disability in the hopes that the child will somehow appear as "normal," it only fosters the eventual and ultimate difficulties the child will face as he tries to be accepted both by and within the community.

The school years for the first time, also present communities within communities to the student with special needs. As each school is a community in and of itself, so too is the classroom, as well as the socially dictated groups of friends that form. These groups include some and exclude others. The most obvious example of this comes in the pre-teen years when the primary requirement for inclusion is normality—as long as there is a peer group that looks and talks like the student, there is acceptance.

Some students are stimulated by the classroom community, yet others are intimidated and withdraw into themselves. During these early years the child first experiences the division within communities, or mini-communities: teachers/students; "smart," (receptive)/"slow" (withdrawn); caregivers/receivers. In other words, complex communities exist within larger communities.

Challenges of a 21st Century Community

We can certainly point to signs of progress in all areas with regard to community partnerships. But interestingly, as the faithful worked to educate and illuminate the subject, society itself became more a group of individuals and less of a community. As Bogdan and Taylor found, society becomes a collection of people "isolated and estranged" from one another.[1] Computers with their possibilities have us staring into a screen much of the day. Videos, DVDs, video games, malls and e-mail, although they facilitate communications, can also reduce or even eliminate face-to-face interaction. What might have been a caring, nurturing, and fruitful environment with the potential to be a welcoming one has now turned inward and has itself become dysfunctional. Society is now unprepared to welcome those outside of the "norm," when those deemed within the "norm" can no longer find each other.

The City as Many Communities

Cities are simply multi-faceted communities. They exist to either "supply" or to "demand" an infinite number of services and resources. They absorb smaller communities (e.g., immigrants, homeless, entrepreneurs, artists, tourists, those with special needs . . . . The list is endless. Cities and some large communities paradoxically threaten independence by pulling groups into the anonymity of city life; but, at the same time, they create opportunities for further self-definition and experience. Robert Park and others were some of the first sociologists to analyze that crime and corruption flourish along with art, good politics, inventiveness, abundant services, and opportunities.[2]

1. Robert Bogdan and Steven J. Taylor, *Building Stronger Communities for All: About Community Participation for People with Developmental Disabilities*. A. Tymchuk, K. Charlie Lakin, & R. Luckasson (eds.), *The Forgotten Generation: The Status and Challenges of Adults With Mild Cognitive Limitations*. (p.191). Baltimore: Paul H. Brookes Publishing Co.
2. Robert E. Park, Ernest W. Burgess, R.D. McKenzie. *The City*. (University of Chicago Press, 1925).

A city's vitality provides the setting for a multitude of partnerships for communities of the disabled. As an umbrella for more special communities, the city offers myriad partnerships from employment opportunities, to cultural relationships, educational offerings, sporting venues, etc. Conversely, as a microcosm of the city, the small community offers the same opinions, with more limited scope, but boundless rewards.

CREATING VALUABLE COMMUNITY PARTNERSHIPS: A PRIMER FOR PROVIDERS AND PARENTS. A THREE STEP PROCESS.

Providers that serve people with cognitive disabilities should find themselves not only in the human service field, but also public relations, fund raising, employment and travel services; and volunteer resource centers, as well as social directors, mobility specialists, and community activists. Providers cannot be casual dabblers in these fields, but must be experts. Aside from providing the requisite life skills and employment skills, the provider must also define its mission as a community partner.

Many providers make a mistake by thinking they can survive by merely being good providers. Although that goal is admirable and certainly is at the core of what makes us successful in the field, it is not nearly enough. It is the responsibility of the provider to devote some portion of staff time to the cultivation of community partners. This time can be allocated to the board chair, executive director, program director, or directors of employment services, community living, education, or marketing. In truth, all or any of these professionals need to be a part of the effort to cultivate partnerships. Once linkage is made in the community, it can be introduced into programming.

Step I: Board Selection

In many non-profits, the executive director and chair of the board of directors confer on potential board nominees. The nominating committee will step in, and all will voice their opinions on who might make the most valuable board member. Usually the qualities sought include the ability to give money or knowing someone who can, preferably someone with a high profile name in the community or some particular expertise the board may be deficient in. These are all extremely important, but unfortunately, one quality is often missing: the board should be looking for members who can provide fruitful partnerships in the community that will contribute to the growth and self-esteem of the individuals the agency serves.

Take, for example, the non-profit board of a provider of services to adults with learning disabilities, Agency A. The fiscal year was coming to a close and the nominating committee, which was supposed to have cultivated new members all year, was sorely behind in its work and was just beginning the search for new members. The usual suspects, brought up at every nominating committee of every non-profit in the community, were mentioned: a bank executive, a noted philanthropist, a retired corporate president. A member of the nominating committee quietly mentioned the name of the owner of a neighborhood dry cleaner who happened to have a child with a learning disability. The committee ignored his suggestion, extolling the virtues of the other three nominees. The committee member, after a couple of "ahems," described the drycleaner's community involvements, including scouting, recycling, beautification, and the local small business administration. He was, of course, overruled and the group chose the bank president for his visibility, corporate giving potential and business acumen. The bank president said yes to the board's invitation to join, and the drycleaner was soon after invited to join Board B. She accepted.

Now look at the two boards one year later. The bank president's election made a splash in the newspapers when it was announced, but subsequently he did nothing. He said his bank had to cut back on corporate donations because of poor earnings, and he wasn't hiring anyone for the same reason. He seldom attended meetings because he was always out of town. The board had no recourse but to keep him on, in spite of a policy about missing meetings.

Board B, however, immediately recognized the wisdom of having as one of its members, the dry cleaner, who immediately conceived of a work-study vocational program for the agency's members. She also had experience in mobilizing groups to create a community beautification program and implemented one within the agency; she involved a group of clients in a recycling campaign; and when she won the Chamber of Commerce's Business Person of the Year award, she dedicated it to Agency B.

The community partnerships developed by board member B were significant: she became an employment partner, a civic and recreational partner, a business partner, and a link to the Chamber of Commerce, which had limitless possibilities for the agency. Agency A was left with little or nothing to show for its supposed "coup" in attracting a high profile executive to their board.

Step II: Staff Participation

Cultivation of community partnerships can be found in many different arenas. As a case in point an executive director of an agency for cognitively disabled adults asked that at least one staff member attend the local Chamber of Commerce's after-work networking receptions. This was not an event that had ever proven fruitful in the area of job develop-ment, and the attendees were mostly young singles searching for friends. One winter evening, the supervisor of employment services struck up a conversation with a community liaison from the local community col-lege. Trained well in the art of looking beyond the moment to make future connections, the supervisor asked for the name of a contact to dis-cuss the possibility of a college program for adults with learning disabili-ties. The contact was given, a meeting followed, a partnership began—a partnership that not only initiated an innovative program between the provider and the community college, but also saw a dean of the college join the board. Not bad work for one hour of networking. This partner-ship is described in greater detail further in this chapter.

The staff members of a provider also need to be intrinsically commit-ted to their communities. "Our assumption is that the better you know your community, the easier it will be to help someone become involved in that community."[3] The goal of community partnerships in an organi-zation must be intrinsic—many providers have this goal as part of their mission and philosophy statements. With any profession, especially in human services, one must believe in the service being provided and have a vision for the good it achieves. So it is with believing in the bene-fit of a symbiotic relationship with one's community. Those organiza-tions having successful community programs are those that encourage personal commitments by their staff. If the supervisor of supported liv-ing, has no experience volunteering in the community, if the director of recreation has never been a member of a museum, and if the executive director has never served on a volunteer board of directors, the verbal commitment to the community is just that. The organization must not only encourage its staff to participate in community activities, but allow work time to do so. It should publicize in its newsletters accomplish-ments of its staff outside the organization's walls and find ways to recog-nize community service that will serve as an example and encourage other staff to get involved as well.

Step III: Program Integration

Using the above two criteria will set a provider on a true course toward establishing sound community partnerships. It is critical that the first two steps be followed by a third: to include in the curricula of all the services offered to the individual, those skills necessary to take full advan-tage of community partnerships. Curricula in life skills, employment, and education should all have community-centered components.

---

3. *A Guide to Knowing Your Community*, The Center On Human Policy, School of Education, Syracuse University (*CTAT Field Report,1* [1], Winter 1990, pp. 8-9.)

- *Life Skills*

Program A known for teaching independent living to men and women 18 and older, has developed benchmarks required of each person at various stages of their life skills training. Each benchmark must be achieved before the student can move on to the next level and eventually graduate to his or her own apartment in the community. Progress is assessed at 45 days, six months, one year, 18 months and two years. There are 24 sections in the expectations, covering skills like time management, safety skills, food preparation, and self control. Several sections relate directly to one's ability to recognize, navigate, and enjoy community partnerships.

A section entitled "Demonstrates Appropriate Awareness for Services in the Community," tackles the issues head on. Within that section, the following skills are assessed at the intervals outlined above, and graded by both the residential life skills department and the vocational department. The individual must:

1. Have basic understanding of how to read the newspaper.
2. Be able to use the newspaper to locate community functions.
3. Be able to use newspapers to collect coupons.
4. Use a phone book to find numbers for services in the community.
5. Identify when to call a landlord.
6. Have access to and be aware of local churches, synagogues, and other religious services.
7. Be aware of special interest clubs in the community.
8. Have an understanding of local state services available to assist.

Many of the 24 sections have at least one or two requirements that deal with community skills. For example, the "Communication Skills" section has a number of items:

1. Develop communication skills necessary to acquire community services.
2. Interact appropriately with community workers in order to obtain services.
3. Provide the information needed to obtain a specific service.

A logical place for the underscoring of the importance of a community relationship is within the individual's support team. Including the bus driver, the fast food restaurant manager and the volunteer coordinator at his place of work, is a way not only to reinforce the importance, but to communicate that importance to those members of the community. Educating the community at large is a necessary step in the path to community partnerships.The strategies used to teach the skills and the philosophy are, of course, key, and one method is to integrate the teaching of the skill into the classroom.

- *Education*

A comprehensive education curriculum in an adult program should not only focus on functional academics, and the skills necessary for independent living but should also include various components related to success in the community and introduce them in concert with hands-on life skills training. A curriculum that introduces the skills required to read the newspaper, find a number in the phone book, and pick a place of worship will graduate a person ready to create community partnerships on his own.

Scenario: Louise is a first year student in a two-year residential program. If she successfully meets the expectations for graduation, she will move into her own apartment and become a member of the community. While in the residential program, her core curriculum follows a path that will eventually lead to independence, where she will make decisions on her own about her personal community partnerships. Her classes include those that help her identify her personal choices for community partnerships.

In her first term, Louise is required to take certain courses as pre-requisites to later ones. Her favorite course is Community Resources in which she learns how to identify and use the community resources available to her. She develops a list of services of special interest to her including churches, museums and bowling alleys. She and her class cut coupons from the newspaper, find movies and times, and look for sales at their favorite stores.

In another core class, Louise learns mobility skills to get her back and forth from the community resources she has identified. Learning to read a bus schedule is difficult for even the most accomplished of travelers, but Louise starts with the destination, and with the help of her classroom teacher, traces her journey from beginning to end. Louise chose to begin her partnerships with the local synagogue. Approximately five miles from the program she was attending, it offered her the religious affiliation she wanted, plus social activities and a circle of friends outside her classmates.

In the classroom, she has learned the intricacies of the route; in her mobility class, she has learned the hands-on skills necessary to take the bus; in her social interactions class, she sees examples of acceptable and not-so-acceptable social behavior. Louise is now ready to forge ahead and make a partner.

• *Employment*

Learning the skills to become successful in the world of work is an important component to any independent living program. But it falls short of its true potential without a component that takes classroom skills and applies them to the job. A work-study program that is part of the core curriculum required for a transition to independent living in the community works best.

Scenario: David came to his adult provider after successfully completing high school and earning a certificate of completion. His parents chose a particular adult provider because it offered a wide array of services that would support David for the rest of his life.

Soon after entering the program, David and his parents had an appointment with the Supervisor of Employment services. During their conversation, David's parents were adamant that he go directly to competitive employment because he had worked for his uncle in a retail store for the past two years and had done very well. Despite the supervisor's explanation regarding the need for work-study to both assess David's skills in various areas and to give him a chance to see what it is like to work for someone other than his uncle, the parents were firm.

The program found a job for David in the community at a nearby restaurant. As the parents had instructed, he was given some one-to-one support early in his employment, and then gradually, the support was removed. Soon, the manager of the restaurant placed a call to the employment specialist. It just wasn't working out with David. He was often found loafing on the job; even with training, he did not load the dishwasher correctly and stated he "didn't like to wash dishes"; he often came in late to work and slipped out early.

"How could this be?" asked the parents. Upon further investigation into David's past employment, it was quickly discovered that working for his uncle was definitely not a real-world work experience. David was allowed to come and go whenever he pleased—he had no start time and no quitting time. His tasks were minimal, ranging from getting coffee for the rest of the staff, to shredding papers. It became quite clear all too quickly that there was no job description and no requirements for the job.

Had David joined his friends in the program at the work-study site, a major retail chain store, he would have learned that a good employee must arrive on time; perform the tasks required; get along with fellow employees; take pride in his work; and not leave until the shift was over. The partnership that the provider had forged with the retail store also allowed the employer to make ongoing assessments of each student's progress, complete with commendations and recommendations. Only when the work-study employer felt the student could move on to competitive employment did that step take place.

Teaching employment skills is often best taught both in—and out—of the classroom. Community partnerships have unique ways of teaching that are far from traditional ones. Sometimes with of all of the classroom training, all the practice bus runs, and all the role-playing that occur before a new experience is tackled, the intangible and unteachable skill of reacting appropriately when something unplanned happens, falls short of what society expects.

Conforming to social norms is often the skill that is most difficult for an individual with a social or intellectual impairment to master. An example is Felicity. Felicity had been in her special education class during her elementary and high school years. After receiving her special education certificate at the conclusion of her formal education, she was fortunate to be able to sign on with a day-program provider of employment services and life skills. The provider worked to individualize her program, giving her special attention and extra hours of vocational coaching in the areas where she needed them most, namely interpersonal skills and hygiene. In the classroom, if her work was not perfect, she was given an opportunity to do it again.

During her work-study program, she was met each day by an employment specialist who reviewed with her whether she was dressed appropriately for the job, whether her grooming was up to standard, and what her responsibilities would be for the day. The specialist then transported her to the job site and stayed with her for the entire work time. After a period of time, Felicity's support team determined that she was ready to try competitive employment, and they were successful in securing a part-time position at a local drug store whose staff knew the clients of the agency well and had supported their schedules in the past. One work day, Felicity began yelling at a fellow employee. Her employment specialist calmed her down and removed her from the environment. When they returned, the manager of the store confronted Felicity reminding her that this was a place of business and Felicity had frightened a customer and fellow employees. If there were another incident , she would be fired.

Felicity began to learn that this work experience—in the greater community—was quite different from her nurturing experiences in the classroom and with her life skills instructors. It took a willing and caring partner to help her learn, but having it be a community partner made all the difference to Felicity's learning experience.

PARTNERSHIPS THAT SUCCEED

Fortunately, both urban and suburban areas have plenty of opportunities for partnerships that work. Each area has its advantages and disadvantages. Generally, given the preliminary groundwork described above for both the provider and the person seeking the partnership, most can be fruitful.

- *Partnerships That Teach*

Partnerships that teach are primarily in the educational area. We will look at those first. For example, as described earlier, a program for adults with cognitive disabilities developed a partnership with the local community college. The program provides its cognitively impaired students with a real college experience and an invaluable community partnership. The program is designed to introduce students to college life so they may gain the confidence to further their education. Students visit the two campuses of the college to meet with instructors and staff, tour the facilities, and observe classes. They attend their own classes run by the agency's own teachers and eventually have instruction on filling out a college application.

As with the best of community partnerships, this one has all the ingredients of a winner. First, the experience on a college campus—eating in the cafeteria, being issued a student ID, walking the halls with the other students, graduating—gives each participant the self-esteem that an academic environment provides. Second, the partnership naturally flowed into other opportunities within the greater community: the college hired a supported employment crew from the agency to work in their cafeteria; one of the professors guest-lecturing to the agency's students is also an expert in Tai Chi and agreed to teach a class in the agency's continuing education program; and the dean of the college joined the board of the agency. But perhaps the greatest benefits of a college partnership for individuals with disabilities are realized when the program ends. The friendships, knowledge that success can come in an academic setting, and self-esteem that can only come when success is acknowledged in the community, are attainable through this partnership. As these students progress on their path to independence, the college partnership will always be representative of yet another obstacle overcome.

The public school system of New Haven, Connecticut, received a federal grant to establish a Community Classroom program for some of its students. Based on the premise that an age-appropriate setting is far more beneficial than allowing older high school students in the special education program to be in the same classrooms as freshmen, the Community Classroom takes their students away from the four walls of the high school community. One of two sites being utilized is the Jewish Home for the Aged.

Each morning the students either take buses or their own transportation to the Home or arrive at their high school to access designated transportation. They attend classes in the morning and then begin job shadowing within the home. Many jobs within the setting interest the students and prepare them for employment after the program ends. Getting hand-over-hand training in skills necessary for janitorial positions, and jobs in food service and grounds maintenance, is invaluable. Even during the program, students are encouraged to seek outside employment, the eventual hoped-for outcome.

Although just in its first year, the program has already been successful in not only establishing a valuable community partnership for the school system and the students, but also opening doors to future employment and teaching vocational skills that will be good for a lifetime.

Partnerships That Employ

Probably when one thinks of community partnerships in this context, one thinks of employment partnerships. In fact, these links are among the most numerous among providers and often best serve the needs of all parties. We have touched briefly on the differences, or lack thereof, between opportunities available in urban versus suburban settings. One opportunity for an employment link to the community is that of neighborhood action groups. If cities are just many neighborhoods, then a small town is simply fewer neighborhoods. Both have various neighborhood groups looking for participants. (It should be noted here that for the purposes of this chapter, no distinction will be made between paid and volunteer employment. Both reflect community partnerships.) Involvement in such a group is usually easy and can range in benefit from skill enhancement, to social opportunities and friendships. Neighborhood groups often represent worthwhile causes. An example in our neighborhood was the effort to designate it as an historical district. Although much of the work involved lobbying and filing of paperwork, it also involved putting up fliers, gathering the merchants in the neighborhood together for information sessions, collating mailings, and keeping the neighborhood looking good for on-the-spot inspections. The clients of a nearby community provider became a valuable part of the effort. They were able to see a project from beginning to end and be successful at all that they were assigned; they made friends who lived nearby and with whom they could socialize outside the community group's activities. Most importantly, they were valued for what they contributed.

The National Foundation for Teaching Entrepreneurship (NFTE) had its beginnings as a means for inner-city, at-risk youth to learn the skills necessary to start and run their own businesses. Rewarded with overall success in high schools all over the country and resulting acclaim and national visibility, NFTE was approached by a provider of services to adults with cognitive disabilities to get permission to modify the NFTE curriculum to serve its population. With innovation being the stuff of dreams for NFTE, they of course said yes.

The provider received funding from a private foundation (another community partner) to purchase all necessary materials to revise and offer the new curriculum to its students. It also received funding to offer its clients internships after the NFTE curriculum was completed, a totally new idea for the organization. The classroom work took about eight months, and then the internships began. Because the idea of teaching entrepreneurship to learning disabled adults as a way to enhance their self-esteem and their employment skills was a new concept to area employers, they were eager to sign on. (Of course, the fact that the salaries of their employees were subsidized by a grant didn't hurt their enthusiasm.)

The internships were perfect. A cleaning service; a graphic design shop; a lawyer's office; a moving company, just to name a few. As you might imagine, the training and experience gained in the internships were extremely valuable and helped the clients get good jobs later on, but the real value was in the partnerships that developed. NFTE became an ongoing advisor and partner in both the provider's education curriculum and employment department, and the employers became a part of the organization's Business Advisory Group and lifelong supporters of the students it employed. Ongoing employment followed with some and others were available to give advice on the region's economic and employment climate.

Cultural Partnerships

An advantage to a city location for an individual or provider is the greater availability of cultural opportunities. While most post-secondary options offer recreation programs, not all offer the opportunity for individuals to become a part of the cultural society in which they live. For the parent exploring options, delving below the surface of marketing materials into the programs offered by a provider is key, and the area of cultural partnerships is no exception. Cities offer many cultural venues including theaters, museums, musical performances, cultural clubs, and churches. A recreation program that offers interest groups as part of its program paves the way for cultural involvement. For instance, an interest group might get together once a week and share its favorite folk music CDs, but members would also attend a concert, talk about it afterward, and perhaps meet some of the performers or write a fan letter. An interest group in painting meets once a week to try their hands with a paint-brush and easel.

A transition program recently teamed up with a local private college that was known for its drama program. The college found itself short on stage-hands, and the program had received a grant to establish a comprehensive drama program—a perfect match. The Drama Club participated in the production of Off-Off Broadway plays from auditions through to final performances. Students volunteered as stage crew members, which included giving cues to actors, assisting with set construction, make-up, props, and costume changes as well as general stage management. The college program got the help it needed, and the students gained confidence and self-esteem and experienced the excitement of being a part of a theatrical production as well as being on a college campus. Certainly, a provider situated in a more suburban setting also offers its own brands of cultural partnership opportunities. Museums and theaters are often not far away and with technology shrinking the globe, many options are at our fingertips, wherever we may live.

CONCLUSION: CHOICE OR CHANCE—THE ULTIMATE DECISION

Starting at birth, the parents of an intellectually challenged child must make decisions that will ultimately affect how he or she navigates the world. The variety of choices is influenced by the degree to which parents explore the options available to their children. Leaving the future of an individual with a disability to chance will lead to a life devoid of the opportunities available in a community rich with partnership opportunities.

A number of providers offer transition services, but the wise parents place importance on the availability of community partnerships when making a choice. Savvy providers should make a special effort to give visibility to community partnerships that have contributed to their clients' success. They should list their boards of directors along with community affiliations to tout an array of community commitments. The knowledgeable parents should ask to see the agency newsletters or annual reports to check for any mention of staff participation in community projects. In addition, and most importantly, close scrutiny of the agency's programming is vital. The provider must offer participation in and education about community activities as part of its core programming: life skills, education and employment.

The rewards of community partnerships are many. Although we have focused on the benefits of community partnerships to individuals with cognitive disabilities in this context, we must also remind ourselves that the value of community partnerships goes far beyond the child or adult for whom it is designed. One who has experienced the true benefit of a community partnership at school, club, or place of worship sees the potential for success among individuals with learning disabilities.

Inclusion benefits everyone. The child or the client is not the only beneficiary: we all are. Community inclusion via partnerships emphasizes "sameness," "oneness," and the universality of the human experience.

Inclusive community partnerships promote democratic thinking and civil rights, and also help fight against the social ills that come from separation, unfamiliarity, and a lack of understanding. We must remind ourselves that community partnerships help everyone better understand the world of these courageous people who struggle everyday with day-to-day tasks the rest of us take for granted.

Chapter Nine

Transitional Issues and Strategies For Change:
Becoming the Successful Young Adult

Deborah A. Brodbeck, M.S.

President of Beacon College in Leesburg, Florida

The purpose of this chapter is to identify transitional issues that create barriers to success for students with learning disabilities and high-light strategies that will assist them in developing the necessary skills for academic achievement and attainment of personal goals. A review of the literature has shown that students with learning disabilities often have difficulty with transitions (Brinckerhoff, McGuire, & Shaw, 2002; Gajar, 1998; Getzel, Stodden, & Briel, 2001; Vogel & Adelman,1992). Primary challenges are student readiness, social interaction, problem solving, time management and organizational skills, and the ability to determine and accomplish personal goals. Each of these challenges will be described, along with strategies for facilitating more successful transitions, independent functioning, and the capacity for self-determination.

Transitional issues for students with learning disabilities often create barriers for successful attainment of academic and personal goals. Many of these barriers are inherent in just having a learning disability. Developing effective interventions on a secondary level will facilitate achieving academic success in higher education, just as transitional planning from college to the workplace will assist students in achieving their professional goals.

Student Readiness

For the college bound student with learning disabilities there are basic readiness skills that facilitate a successful transition to college. These readiness skills are:

- Self-awareness of cognitive strengths and weaknesses.
- Knowledge of academic strengths and weaknesses.
- Self-acceptance of the learning disability.
- Ability to self-advocate.
- Effective use of resources and accommodations.
- Motivation to succeed.
- Honest and realistic appraisal of the level of services required for academic success.

The readiness skills defined above foster the success of students with learning disabilities. However, most secondary students with learning disabilities may not have the self-awareness to employ these skills. Many college-able students with learning disabilities often do not understand the nature of their disability (Cowen, 1993) and lack the independence required for meeting the demands of a collegiate environment (Manganello, 1990). Their self-awareness may only extend to identifying what they can't do, while lacking the basic understanding of their cognitive strengths and what they can do. Many students may require counseling or guidance in accepting their disability (Cowen, 1993) and overcoming dysfunctional compensations that may lead to denial or overconfidence (Ness & Price, 1990).

How may families and secondary school professionals partner together in facilitating the development of these critical skills and the self-awareness that fosters success? The following suggestions may assist in addressing these issues with college bound students:

- When students are evaluated, make sure they are an integral part in the conferencing assessment results. Concentrate on the student developing an awareness of his/her cognitive strengths and weaknesses. Highlight how these strengths and weaknesses affect their acquisition of academic skills. Too often, the students are left out of the loop, or may leave a conference with no real understanding of what the assessment results truly mean. This does a disservice to the student; the most important participant in the conferencing process. The goal of any assessment process must be to contribute to the student's self-awareness and the ability to develop an understanding as to what strengths the student may employ in the learning process.

- As the secondary students receive support services, have the support service professionals reinforce learning strategies that work for the individual student. An emphasis on understanding the student's learning style and developing compensatory strategies that utilize his/her strengths to compensate for the disability that interferes with the learning process will enhance the capacity to learn.

- Assist the students in acceptance of their learning disability and develop a comprehensive understanding of the barriers to the acquisition of the skills necessary to compensate.

- Provide situations that require self-advocacy. Do not provide solutions; rather guide the students through a process in which they can take ownership. In this manner, the student will be able to generalize these strategies to new situations and will develop the self-confidence and the ability to take risks.

- Professionals working with the student should reinforce effective use of learning resources and appropriate accommodations. Students with learning disabilities should not graduate from high school with the concept of entitlement. They should have acquired the skills necessary to assist them in accommodating their learning disability and understand the resources and/or strategies that will help them in achieving success in the academic arena.

- Develop a plan and let the student work the plan. Setting short-term goals will develop an understanding that goal directed behaviors render results. Students can set goals initially for a term, followed by planning goals for the academic year. This exercise will provide the student practical experience in goal setting, which will assist him/her in achieving successful outcomes later in life.

- Both the parents and the student must have realistic goals and be able to clearly define the academic support required for success. There must be a goodness of fit between program design of support services and the individual needs of the student. This can only be achieved through a realistic and honest appraisal of the delivery of services that are best suited to the student.

Self-awareness, self-acceptance, and the ability to self-advocate are the underpinnings of successful academic outcomes. The importance of the appropriate use of accommodations and the ability to plan, assists the secondary student in developing the skills necessary for success in the collegiate environment. Frequently, students with special needs lack the self-awareness and readiness skills for a successful transition to college. They may be college-able, but do not have the basic readiness skills that provide for a successful transition. It is important that both parents and professionals develop an awareness of these prerequisite skills that are so critical in achieving the postsecondary goals of their student.

Social Interactions/Social Problem Solving

One of the greatest challenges in the transition to postsecondary education is the challenge of living independent of family and special educators. Students are frequently confronted with daily decision-making and social problem solving while transitioning to independence on a college campus. This is a primary concern for parents, and a frequent barrier to success. Students with learning disabilities, inherently have maturational lags that affect the acquisition of age appropriate social skills and effective problem solving. Students are judged by their chronological age, while struggling with the social skills of an individual much younger. Maturational lags are compounded by a difficulty in understanding social cues, language processing deficits, and impulsivity. "College is an important time of growth and development, a time of transition from dependence to independence, and [this] is especially so for individuals with disabilities" (Benshoff, Kroeger, & Scalia, 1990, p. 43). Psychosocial adjustment is essential in accomplishing the transition to young adulthood and independence. Therefore, secondary and postsecondary service providers need to prioritize their delivery of services by fostering social skills development and independence.

The ability to understand social nuances and integrate social cues may be a challenge for the young adult with learning disabilities. These skills may need to be extrinsically taught in order to increase social awareness and the capacity to modify behavior to the social context. Developing the capacity to be more aware of the social environment and engaging in appropriate social interactions will ease the transition in unfamiliar circumstances.

Strategies that assist in developing social skills will enhance social interactions and the ability to problem solve, while preparing students for successful transitions for independent living. The following strategies may direct attention to assisting students in acquiring these skills:

- Secondary students need to acquire work experience, even if the positions are volunteer opportunities. The work environment allows the student to develop self-discipline and a better understanding of appropriate social interactions in a more formal environment. Having to respond to the parameters of the work environment will assist the maturation process, while providing valuable experiences that contribute to social development.

- Families and professionals should provide practical experience in problem-solving. Strategies for identifying problems and problem resolution will lead to a greater level of independence. Too often, students are provided solutions and are not active participants in the process. This leaves students dependent on others for problem resolution and they are denied the opportunity for developing a repertoire of effective problem-solving strategies. As a result, students become dependent on others to resolve their problems, and acquire a *learned helplessness* in social situations.

- In some situations, families or counselors may have to foster social development by encouraging the student to participate in social groups. These may be school-based or affiliated with athletic, church, or community groups.

- Allow students to become actively engaged in decision-making. Foster situations that require the student to make a decision. The ability to problem-solve is a function of practice, which leads to self-confidence derived from real life situations.

- It may be necessary to identify inappropriate social behavior and prompt the student each time the behavior occurs. Doing so will help the student develop an awareness of the frequency of the behavior and develop strategies to self-regulate. This will enhance internal control and lead to improved socialization and more socially appropriate independent behavior.

All of the above strategies will foster both the maturation process and social skill development. Every social encounter involves some level of problem-solving, which allows the student to develop more effective social interactions through experience.

Frequently, parents and professionals provide solutions, make the decisions, and do not foster the student's involvement in the problem-solving process. Without the practical experiences of problem-solving and generating solutions, it is difficult for students with learning disabilities to mature to independent functioning. When they transition to college, they will demonstrate poor decision-making and lack the prerequisite skills to cope with the independence indicative of the collegiate environment.

Time Management/Organizational & Study Skills

The areas of time management and organizational skills will be tested immediately upon arrival on the college campus. The collegiate environment does not offer the security of a seven-hour academic day. Classes are scheduled generally in one and half hour time blocks twice a week. A student could have days that are heavily scheduled, followed by a day with no classes. Students with learning disabilities transitioning from secondary school often have difficulty organizing their time and meeting the demands of a college schedule. The ability to manage time and organize not only class assignments, but class schedules will present special challenges for students with learning disabilities. These students often lack the skills required for time management and may not have acquired effective organizational skills while in high school. Too often, students with learning disabilities are directed rather than being active participants in organizing their time and assignments. Thus, they leave high school dependent on others to organize their time and assignments. Aune (1991), conducted research demonstrating that only fifteen percent of students in a secondary program reported being taught learning strategies during the year. Subsequently, the students lacked study strategies that are the prerequisite skills for academic success and independent functioning.

Suggestions for facilitating acquisition of these critical time management and organizational skills are:

- Educational support programs on a secondary level are enhanced when students become active participants in developing their own learning strategies and time management skills. Professionals should foster independence by having students become actively involved in time management and task completion strategies. Frequently, educators "tend to organize, prioritize, and break down assignments for the students rather than with the students" (DuChossois & Michaels, 1994, p. 87). This establishes co-dependency and leaves students with no internal mechanisms to accomplish tasks or effectively manage their time.

- Families may assist in this process by having their student develop strategies for completing tasks assigned in the home or when they seek assistance in homework. Parents may initially guide their secondary student through time management strategies for task completion, but need to have the student actively engaged in the process. Dictating procedures and timelines does not produce the ability to generalize the experience, rather the students may become dependent on the parent as the external locus for time management and task completion.

- Families and professionals can partner together in assisting students in developing strategies that work for them and understanding how to manage their time and assignments. This only emerges through active participation by the student. Students need to develop a heightened awareness of what approach to learning works best for them. This will foster independence while increasing confidence in an academic environment.

Goal Orientation & Accomplishing the Plan

Frequently, students with learning disabilities have limited experience in goal setting, which affects self-directed behavior and attainment of personal goals. This may be a function of having been directed and not having been an active participant in setting personal goals and the development of strategies that accomplish a plan to achieve these goals. Experience in developing a plan and working the plan to achieve goals provides practice in critical thinking, development of problem-solving skills when plans need to be modified, and development of self-confidence, which is the foundation of self-determination.

Both school professionals and parents can partner together in providing practice in goal setting and developing a plan to accomplish the goals. The experience of achieving initial goals that may even be minimal will provide the practical experience that is a learning platform for accomplishing even greater challenges. If a student is deprived of the opportunity to determine personal goals and the development of strategies to accomplish a plan to achieve those goals, the transition to adulthood may be an unsure one.

Suggestions for facilitating goal orientation and the attainment of personal goals are:

- School professionals and special educators can easily integrate practice in goal setting and the ability to develop a plan to accomplish the goal in classroom or resource room activities. There are a myriad of opportunities for goal setting in the academic environment, and by experiencing success in these areas, the attainment of goals becomes real. The student "owns" the success, which in turn leads to improved self-confidence and the ability to take risks to attain new horizons.

- Parents may also foster goal setting in the home environment. Having the student develop personal goals within the family environment may also facilitate a more integrated home life. Socialization begins within the home environment and setting personal goals in the context of family will allow the student with learning disabilities to begin exploring how to achieve success in a social environment. This provides practical experience in social problem-solving and attainment of a meaningful life in the context of others.

- Goal setting and the ability to "work the plan" also provides the opportunity to think critically, problem-solve, and develop self-discipline in accomplishing the goal. Promoting the intrinsic ability for goal setting and developing the capacity to work a plan to accomplish the goal fosters independence, self-determination, and the capacity to engage in adult behavior.

- To prepare for the transition for college, parents and guidance counselors must work closely with the student in developing a plan for screening colleges and determining realistic goals. Students must seek a college setting that will facilitate their learning and have the appropriate support services. This process should begin early in the student's postsecondary program so that the student is adequately prepared for a college curriculum and is realistic regarding appropriate support services (Cowen,1993).

Self-Determination

In reviewing the literature regarding transitional processes for students with learning disabilities, there is a core belief that another fundamental component of successful transition from postsecondary school to college, then college to the workplace is self-determination. The ability to act with self-determination requires self-awareness, the ability to set and accomplish goals, creative problem-solving, self-advocacy, and the ability to self-evaluate and modify behavior (Martin & Marshall, 1996). The development of readiness skills and time management/organizational skills with the capacity to determine and accomplish goals lays the foundation for academic success. However, psychosocial development, self-awareness, and the ability to think critically and evaluate behavior provide the capacity to attain personal goals and develop the skills necessary for self-determination and realization of personal potential.

To become a successful adult, one must have a self-awareness that leads to self-determination.

> People who are self-determined use a comprehensive and reasonably accurate knowledge of themselves and their strengths and limitations to act in such a manner to capitalize on this knowledge. This self-knowledge and self-understanding forms through experience with and interpretation of one's environment and is influenced by evaluations of significant others, reinforcement, and attributions of one's own behavior (Wehmeyer, Agran, & Hughes, 1998, p. 274).

Contributing to a student's self-awareness provides the self-knowledge and understanding that are the prerequisites for self-determination, which provides the foundation for successful transitions. A student's ability to become self-determined allows for the opportunity to achieve personal goals and realize one's potential in the transition to adulthood. Both parents and school professionals can foster the development of self-determination by providing opportunities in the environment that facilitate self-awareness. The following strategies will assist a student in realizing his/her potential and foster the self-awareness to determine goal directed behavior:

- School professionals should assist students in understanding both cognitive strengths and weaknesses. Highlighting what works for a student regarding learning strategies and study skills will enhance a student's ability to utilize these strategies and generalize these skills in a variety of settings. For example, when achieving a good test grade, have the student identify the strategies and/or study environment employed and reinforce the use of these strategies. When achieving a poor grade, identify the error pattern and study methodology. What was different? What was the same? How did the learning disability interfere with performance? How does a student apply what works in one circumstance to enhance performance in another?

- Parents may also assist students by highlighting strengths that are observed in the home environment. Linking these strengths to generalized circumstances will also improve the self-awareness and confidence that are the underpinnings of self-determined behavior. For example, a parent may recognize that their student has a good rote memory for facts. This ability may be linked to study skills and even employment that requires recall of facts as part of the job prerequisite (e.g., marketing or sales).

Ensuring that any conferencing of an educational evaluation includes the student as an active participant, as outlined previously, is a necessary initial step in contributing to a student's self-awareness. This improves self-knowledge and understanding of the learning disability, and more importantly, the strengths that a student may employ to develop effective learning strategies. The student must possess an accurate assessment of strengths and weaknesses in order to have the capacity to self-determine behavior, develop realistic goals, and achieve their potential.

Conclusion

Students with learning disabilities are increasingly pursuing postsecondary education, which will require a comprehensive planning process to facilitate a successful transition. Developing an effective partnership of all parties concerned with the transition: the student, the family, and school professionals will contribute to achieving the goal of a smooth transition from secondary to postsecondary programs.

Developing strategies that enhance the secondary student's basic readiness and time/management skills, social-emotional status, and self-awareness will contribute to achieving a successful transition to college. Both the parents and school professionals can facilitate the student's self-awareness and comprehensive understanding of his/her learning disability, which are the cornerstones of becoming a successful young adult who leads a self-determined and independent lifestyle.

In addition, transition to a college campus may also be facilitated by:

- Attending the college for a summer session to familiarize the student with learning disabilities with the campus facilities and location of classrooms, the library, counseling and academic advisement offices, student services office, and educational support services center.

- Visiting the college campus prior to the beginning of the term if a student can't attend a summer term.
- Registering for a reduced course load for the initial semester. Scheduling classes that are conducive to optimizing the student's performance. If the student is a late sleeper, avoid scheduling a lot of early morning classes!
- Contacting the Office of Disability Support Services regarding accommodations prior to the start of classes in order to ensure their availability at the beginning of the semester.

References

CHAPTER 5

Garbarino, James, Ph.D. (1999). *Lost Boys: Why Our Sons Turn Violent and How We Can Save Them.* Simon and Schuster, Inc.

Levine, Arthur and Cureton, Jeanette (1998). *When Hope and Fear Collide: A Portrait of Today's College Student,* Jossey-Bass.

Levine, Mel, M.D. (2002). *A Mind At A Time.* Simon and Schuster, Inc.

Smith, Corinne and Strick (1997). Lisa, *Learning Disabilites: A to Z A Parent's Complete Guide to Learning Disabilities from Preschool to Adulthood.* Simon and Schuster, Inc.

Smith, Sally (1991). *Succeeding Against the Odds: How the Learning Disabled Can Realize Their Promise.* G.P. Putnam's Sons.

CHAPTER 6

Anderson, A. N. (2001). Why bother? How persons with disabilities benefit as volunteers. *Impact* 14 (2) 4–5.

Anderson, S. (1998). Service learning: A national strategy for youth development. *The Communication Network.*

Franks, J. (1986). A program for sighted, blind, low vision and disabled volunteers. *Journal of Visual Impairment & Blindness, 80* (3), 631–632.

Gobel, S. & Flynn J. (1995). Not another board meeting: Guides to building inclusive decision making–groups. Salem, OR: Oregon Developmental Disabilities Council.

Graff, L.L., & Vedell, J. A. (2003). "It Shouldn't Be This Difficult": The views of agencies and persons with disabilities on supported volunteering. *The Journal of Volunteer Administration, 21* (1), 9–24.

Kirby, D. (2001). Emerging answers: Research findings on programs to reduce teen pregnancy. Washington, DC: National Campaign to Prevent Teen Pregnancy.

Krajewski, J. & Callahan, J. (1998). Service-learning: A strategy for vocational training of young adults with special needs. *The Journal For Vocational Special Needs Education, 21* (1) 34–38.

Miller, K. D., Schleien, S.J., & Bedini, L. A. (2003). Barriers to the inclusion of volunteers with developmental disabilities. *The Journal of Volunteer Administration, 21* (1), 25–30.

Miller, K. D., Stallion, S. J., Rider, C., Hall, C., Rote, M., & Dorsally, J. (2002). Inclusive volunteering: Benefits to participants and community. *Therapeutic Recreation Journal, 36* (3), 247–259.

Muscott, H. et. al. (1999). Teaching character education to students with behavioral and learning disabilities through mentoring relationships. *Education and Treatment of Children, 22* (3), 373–390.

Morgan, W., & Streb, M. (2001). Building citizenship: How student voice in service learning develops civic values. *Social Science Quarterly, 82* (1), 155–169.

Murry, J. (2001). Finding a good match: Questions for volunteers and organizations to ask. *Impact 14* (2) 9.

Rosenberg, S.L., Mckeon, L.M., & Dinero, T. E., (1999). Positive peer solutions: One answer for the rejected student. *Phi Delta Kappan, 81*, 114–118.

Safrit, R.D. (2002). Developing effective teen-adult partnerships through volunteerism: Strengthening empathy, engagement, empowerment, and enrichment. *The Journal of Volunteer Administration, 20* (4), 21–26.

Westheimer, J., & Kahne, J. (2000). Report to the Surdna Board. D.V.I. New York: Surdna Foundation.

CHAPTER 9

Aune, E. (1991). A transitional model for postsecondary-bound students with learning disabilities. *Learning Disabilities Research and Practice, 6*, 177–187.

Benshoff, J. J., Kroeger, S. A., & Scalia, V. A. (1990). Career maturity and academic achievement in college students with disabilities. *Journal of Rehabilitation, 56* (2), 40–44.

Brinckerhoff, L. C., McGuire, J. M., & Shaw, S. F. (2002). *Postsecondary education and transition for students with learning disabilities* (2nd ed.). Austin, TX: Pro-Ed.

Cowen, S. (1993). Transition planning for the LD college-bound students. In S.A. Vogel & P. B. Adelman (Eds.), *Success for college students with learning disabilities*, (39–56). New York: Springer-Verlag.

DuChossois, G., & Michaels, C. (1994). Postsecondary education. In C. A. Michaels (Ed.), *Transition strategies for persons with learning disabilities*, (79–117). San Diego: Singular.

Gajar, A. (1998). Postsecondary education. In F. Rausch & J. Chadsey (Eds.), *Beyond high school: Transition from school to work*, (383–405). Belmont, CA: Wadsworth.

Getzel, E. E., Stodden, R. A., & Briel, R. W. (2001). Pursuing postsecondary education opportunities for individuals with disabilities. In P. Wehman (Ed.), *Transition Strategies for young people with disabilities.* (3rd ed)., 247–259. Baltimore: Brookes

Martin, J., & Marshall, L. (1996). Infusing self-determination instruction into the IEP and transition process. In D. Sands & M. Wehmeyer (Eds.), *Self-determination across the life-span*, 215–236. Baltimore: Brookes.

Manganello, R. (1990). The learning disabled college student: Balancing the 3 Rs and the 3 Ds. *Latest Developments: A publication for the learning disabilities special interest group.* Columbus, OH: AHHSSPPEE.

Ness, J., & Price, L.A. (1990). Meeting the psychosocial needs of adolescents and adults with LD. *Intervention in School and Clinic, 26*(1), 16–21.

Vogel, S., & Adelman, P. (1992). The success of college students with learning disabilities: Factors related to education attainment. *Journal of Learning Disabilities, 25*, 430–441.

Wehmeyer, M., Agran, M., & Hughes, C. (1998). *Teaching self-determination to students with disabilities.* Baltimore: Brookes.